# WAKING UP
# AMERICAN

## COMING OF AGE BICULTURALLY

first-generation women reflect on identity

edited by Angela Jane Fountas

**Waking Up American:** Coming of Age Biculturally

An earlier version of "Lone Stars" by Lan Tran appeared in *Falling Backwards: Stories of Fathers & Daughters* (Hourglass Books, 2004). It was first published in *The Chattahoochee Review*, Vol. 22, No. 4. Copyright © 2002 by Lan Tran. Reprinted with permission of the author.

An earlier version of "Raising the Mango" by Angela M. Balcita appeared in *River Styx Magazine*, 68 (Fall 2004): 1–8. Reprinted with permission of the author.

An earlier version of "Palindrome" by Lisa Swanstrom appeared in the Knoxville Writers' Guild's *Migrants & Stowaways: An Anthology of Journeys* (2004). Reprinted with permission of the author.

Published by
Seal Press
An Imprint of Avalon Publishing Group, Incorporated
1400 65th Street, Suite 250
Emeryville, CA 94608

AVALON
publishing group incorporated

ISBN-10: 1-58005-136-7
ISBN-13: 978-1-58005-136-1

9 8 7 6 5 4 3 2 1

Library of Congress Cataloging-in-Publication Data
Waking up American : coming of age biculturally / [edited by] Angela Jane Fountas.
p. cm.
ISBN 1-58005-136-7
1. Children of immigrants—United States. 2. Women—United States. 3. Biculturalism—United States. I. Fountas, Angela Jane.
HQ792.U5W34 2005
305.48'8'00973—dc22
2005011765

Cover and interior design by Amber Pirker
Printed in the United States of America by Berryville
Distributed by Publishers Group West

# CONTENTS

# INTRODUCTION

I USED TO WALK PAST a Vietnamese restaurant that sold *pho*, beef noodle soup, on the way to my bus stop after work. I never saw any customers inside, just two Asian children, a boy and a girl, about four and six years old, and their young parents busy behind the counter. The children sat on their knees at one of the tables, coloring or drawing their worlds, or so I imagined.

One week, the girl sat outside on a crate with a box of See's school-fundraising chocolate bars and a sign that read $1.00. I walked past on Monday and smiled, in a hurry to catch my bus. On Tuesday, I stopped and bought one; she smiled back, sitting quietly next to her sign. I bought a second chocolate bar on Wednesday. After the girl shyly said "thank you," she ran inside the shop calling out something I couldn't understand to her parents.

I grew up, in part, in my family's diner, so I felt a kinship with this Vietnamese girl. But she also reminded me of the divide I had sometimes felt growing up. My father emigrated from Greece in 1958 and married my mother, an American, in 1962. This little Vietnamese girl was able to communicate with both of her parents in their native tongue. Up until the age of twenty-seven, I could not. At home, we spoke English; at the diner, my father and his siblings spoke Greek. I have been forever curious about girls like me who grew up biculturally and make their home in the United States. And this anthology is my way of satisfying this curiosity: Where are you from? Who have you become?

Why this curiosity about women, specifically? The reason is simple. I am the second of four sisters, and although I have two brothers, they didn't enter my world until I was a teenager. My mother is one of seven sisters. Most of my memories from childhood are of my mother, her sisters, and my sisters. My father, like most immigrants, worked long hours so that his children would have more than he had growing up. So, in many ways, mine was a female-centric upbringing. And my adolescence, like many girls', was overshadowed by a desire to fit in, which was complicated by the expectations my father and his family brought with them from Greece. In collecting these essays, I wanted to see how others traversed this terrain to come out whole on the other end.

According to the 2002 U.S. Census Bureau report, one in five residents is either foreign-born or first-generation, the highest level in U.S. history. Americans' collective consciousness is imprinted with images and stories of famine ships crossing the Atlantic, Asian immigrant laborers feeding the gold rush frenzy, Mexican immigrants heading north to escape the turmoil of the revolution, European immigrants passing through Ellis Island. All important stories.

*Waking Up American* collects essays by women from a new wave of first-generation Americans, including those whose stories begin after the Immigration and Nationality Act of 1952 was passed. This act eliminated national origin, race, or ancestry as a basis for denying immigration, ridding the law of its discriminatory elements. This change in immigration law, which grew out of the civil rights movement, resulted in a shift in immigration from developed Western countries to developing countries, such as those in Asia and Latin America.

"First generation" by definition covers two groups of people: immigrants and those whose parents are immigrants. This book expands on this definition to include women like me, for whom being first generation on one side of the family tree is an inextricable part of their identity.

The writers in this collection have roots in China, Germany, Greece, Haiti, India, Iran, Japan, Mexico, Nicaragua, Nigeria, Pakistan, Panama, the Philippines, Puerto Rico, Russia, and Vietnam.

I literally woke up American, born to a legal alien from Greece and his mostly Irish American wife. Some of the women whose essays are collected in this book are children of immigrants; others immigrated to the United States during childhood. But we all, at one time or another, woke up American, and continue to wake up to what this means.

American equals citizen, but it is also an identifier. What happens when another noun joins it to signify ethnicity or descent? You'll find some of the answers to this question in this book.

In "(Un)American," Patricia Justine Tumang writes about being confronted with her own identity when Kenyans refused to accept that she was either American *or* Asian while in the country for a study-abroad program: "Trying to combine my two cultures was like mixing oil with water—no matter how much I tried to mix my Filipino and American identities, they always separated."

Adolescent girls from all walks of life struggle with identity; first-generation girls struggle with an additional layer of cultural identity. The contributors in this book explore coming to terms with multiple identities while coming of age biculturally. This includes being identified as American while strongly identifying with one's mother country. For some, it includes the additional layers of racial or sexual identity that add to the complexity of being "American."

In "Back in the U.S.S.R." Victoria Gomelsky writes: "All the traits, sayings, and customs I associate with my family—from the moments of superstitious silence we observe before leaving on a trip to the exclamation points that pepper our letters—belong to a larger cultural legacy I abandoned in childhood. Being here is my way of getting it back."

Amy André and Marlene Barberousse-Nikolin, both Haitian American, discuss their "experiences, similarities, and differences in growing up, coming out, and exploring multiple layers of identity" through a recorded conversation in "Up the Mountain from Petionville."

In "Hello Kitty Packs Heat," Tina Lee writes: "Like a chameleon, I adapt my colors to an ever-changing environment because my perception of the world is filtered through three lenses: one Chinese, one American, one female. It's like being a Toyota-esque automobile designed by Chinese engineers specifically to meet American needs, assembled by small-town autoworkers in the heartland adhering to an East/West hybrid set of manufacturing standards, and then marketed to the American consumer as something smart and efficient that'll 'love you long time.'"

These essays are moving, sometimes funny, and always honest.

During adolescence, some of us broke ourselves apart to fit in. And most of us have had to find ways to answer the question, "What are you?" that didn't leave us anything less than whole. Side by side, these statements may sound contradictory, but in many ways first-generation women become whole by halves. To some, we are hyphenated Americans. But to ourselves, we are compound individuals with roots that extend across the seas.

In putting this book out into the world, my intention is to add to the conversation about the ways in which culture and identity shape individual lives and continue to help shape this country. And my hope is that this book will one day make it into the hands of the Vietnamese girl who sold me the chocolate bars and inspire her to write her own story.

Angela Jane Fountas
Seattle, April 2005

# RAISING THE MANGO

### Angela M. Balcita

MANGOES HAVE ALWAYS BEEN familiar to my lips, as if their nectar ran in my blood. I know the slippery texture of their pulp, the tickle of their citrus fragrance. I recognize that mix of sweet and tang heating the corners of my mouth, the tip of my tongue, the insides of my cheeks. I don't recall eating my first mango, seeing one for the first time. For as long as I can remember, there have always been mangoes, as bright as sunflowers, as round as shoulders, in a wooden bowl on our kitchen table.

My family's fascination with mangoes may be slightly excessive. My parents take pride in the fruit much the way the Swiss boast about their

1

chocolates or the way the Colombians talk about their coffee. They insist that the best mangoes come from the Philippines, that their sweetness is something no one can refuse. When they find someone who has never tried a mango, they push the fruit like a drug.

The first boy I ever invite to dinner is clearly entranced by my mother. She is pushing the back of her fork into a slice of ripe mango. With little force, she grinds the fruit into the rice left over on her plate from a dinner of chicken and onions. She uses the mango to wipe her entire plate clean. I warned her about not cooking anything too weird tonight, not stinking up the house with anything too fishy. I asked her to make spaghetti. She laughed in my face. Sitting at the table, I wait for her to embarrass me by saying something wrong, something too foreign.

Her mouth is full as she looks over at the young man. In school, he is nice to me. He talks to me, whereas the other boys look past my flat-chested body and my dark brown skin. "You have the blackest hair I've ever seen." His hair is blond and his skin is pale but he has an Italian last name. His voice is still changing and his legs have not yet caught up to the rest of his body. It doesn't bother my mother that he is not Filipino, but it does help that he is Catholic.

"You never see mango before, huh?" she asks him.

The young man, caught a little off guard by the booming sound of her voice, is on his best behavior. He shyly shakes his head.

"Back home, we call that *mangga*. Mun-GA!" When she tries to teach people Tagalog, her native language, the intensity in her voice increases dramatically, as if the volume will make them understand the words better. From my end of the table, I try to signal her to stop, shaking my head and widening my eyes. *No*, I think to myself, *leave him alone.* I hold my breath and wish that her accent would disappear, but it keeps coming, louder and stronger. She slams her hand down on the table twice for emphasis. "Mun-GA!"

The boy, jumping a little when the table shakes, is perhaps bullied into repeating her words. Softly, he says, "Man-ga."

"Mun-GA!"

She offers him a slice, without the rice, putting a bright orange piece on a clean white plate. I tell him not to eat it because the fibers will get caught in his braces. He takes it anyway, eats it, seems to enjoy it. He smiles as he chews, and I can see the piece of fruit inside the skin of his neck slide down his throat. Later, when we kiss on the front porch, I can taste the mix of metal and mango on my tongue. Kissing me is all I'll let him do. Besides the mango, the feel of his mouth on my neck and on my lips feels wrong, like we're moving too fast. I see the words "sex" and "penis" looming just around the next corner. I tell him we should keep it to hand holding and hanging out for now. When he eventually dumps me for a girl who looks just like him, I think her mother probably offers him casseroles for dinner and vanilla ice cream for dessert, and he probably kisses her neck and touches her boobs in the basement all night until curfew.

As I am growing up, my parents teach me to hunt for mangoes in little specialty shops and markets, places that import them from Mexico or Peru. We seek them out much like we search for oriental stores everywhere we go. The gold-mine places carry it all: mangoes, plantains, Chinese sausage, and bok choy. In our small town just outside Pittsburgh, we rarely find any fruit that has not first passed through Toronto or New York. We don't mind buying the South American mangoes when we find them, but my father never stops talking about the Manila mangoes. "They are smaller, you know, sweeter," he closes his eyes, and I know he's imagining himself back on the islands next to a mango tree. "Yes, and they are yellow. Small as your fist."

When we can't find them fresh, my mother buys jars of pickled mangoes from those oriental stores. In these big glass jars, yellow slices of mango swim in a murky sea of salt and vinegar. They are not meant to be sweet, but slightly sour and with a bit of a crunch. They remind me of the mangoes my uncles in the Philippines offer me before dinner. My uncles eat green mangoes, *mangga hilaw*, which are the exact same fruit as the sweet ones, but picked from the tree before they ripen. These mangoes are still green on the outside, stiff to the touch, and when they are peeled and sliced open, they are not juicy and tender. The slices are crisp and breakable, yellowish green in color. My mother eats the pickled mangoes with a pungent dried-shrimp paste, *bagoong*, spread on top, the smell of which is a cross between sweaty gym socks and the San Francisco wharf.

Eating mangoes like this completely disgusts my father, who thinks that picking mangoes before they are ripe is sinful. Mangoes are his favorite fruit, he'll tell you this twice over. He'll tell you that where he's from, when they are juicy and ripe, they are worth more than gold. They're useless if they are picked before they are mature. Their beauty is in their ripeness. It's crucial to wait until their sugary citrus flavor is ready to gush.

My father came to the States from the Philippines in 1968 on a twenty-two-hour flight from Manila to San Francisco. The box of Manila mangoes he had brought to his seat on the plane had not been any sort of problem until he finally landed at SFO. He tried to explain to the customs officer that the mangoes were for his uncle, who had left the Philippines for the United States two years earlier. He was sure his uncle had missed them.

"Nope," the officer said, emptying the entire box into a regulation-size garbage can.

My father, stunned, began to walk to the desk to get his passport stamped. *But have you ever tried one?* he wanted to ask the officer. *If you ever tried one, you'd know.*


My dreamy boyfriend in college loves it when I tell him stories about my family. He repeats them to his friends at bars, over cigarettes.

"Her father tried to smuggle mangoes from the Philippines," he tells them. He laughs and his long brown dreadlocks fall around his mouth. He is a Buddhist and a biology major. He thinks about running for student government and talks about hiking Mount Everest. He loves when I make him food he's never heard of before, loves the off-the-wall stories about my parents. I tell him about how, when my father was living in Manhattan shortly after arriving in this country, he tried to order lunch meat in a deli in Greenwich Village.

"Boloogna, please," my father said politely.

The big hairy clerk behind the counter looked at him, puzzled, and said, "What? What did you say?"

"Bo-loog-na," my skinny father repeated, intertwining the dark fingers of his bony hands. "May I have some boloogna, please?"

"Boloogna? What in Christ's— ... Oh, wait, do you mean baloney? We call it baloney."

My boyfriend loves this story. "He actually called it bologna? That's great! Who says that?" He wants me to produce more, and I try to please him. I mimic my mother's accent. I make him some of the dishes my mother cooks. I try to teach him some Tagalog words, and he tries hard to remember them.

"*Komo esta?*" he says.

"No. *Kumusta ka?*" I correct him, sounding out the words slowly. I think he just likes to watch me talk. He stares at my lips, lips that I've always tried to hide because they are fat, thick, and purple around the edges. He tells me that I am exotic, that I don't look like any other girl on campus, that even my butt curves a certain way that he can't resist. We kiss in his apartment, where tiny Chinese paper lanterns hang from his ceiling and Buddhas of different sizes fill every corner of the room. He pulls off his embroidered Indian shirt, draws me closer to him. He begs me to crawl on his back and give him a massage.

Pictures of his friends decorate the frame of a mirror over his dresser. In every photo, I am amazed by his piercing blue eyes and his white, toothy smile. He is so pretty that at first I am not bothered by the pictures of old girlfriends on the wall. I don't even mind him talking about them.

"Mai-Lani was a vegetarian . . . pretty good cook, but I was always hoping she'd break down and cook me some chicken fried rice . . . Kimiko was really short, so whenever we kissed, it never really worked out."

He can't get over my family stories. He holds my cheeks in his hands and tells me he wants to bring me home to his family. When I insist on bringing something for dinner, he smiles enthusiastically.

I bring chicken and onions, and fresh mangoes in a small brown sack. They are all a hit, and I think I am, too. His mother talks to me in a soft, gentle tone, and his father sits at the end of the table smiling all through dinner. My boyfriend helps me tell them stories while his little sister touches my black hair.

It's in the kitchen after I help his mother with the dishes that I see him in the corner giggling with his brother. I throw a dishcloth over my shoulder and walk by them to catch the last words of the sentence.

". . . *Yang Pie*," I hear his brother say to him, lifting his eyebrows and jostling him lightly with an elbow.

"*Yang Pie?*" I ask. "What's that?"

"Nothing," they both say, and then walk off in different directions.

Later, in his childhood bedroom, with the Boston Red Sox wallpaper and the red, white, and blue bedspread, I ask him again.

"What is *Yang Pie?*" I ask him softly and intently.

He can't avoid the question this time. He hangs his head low, pushes his hair over his shoulder. "It's an Asian porno movie," he says quietly. "Just a joke," he says. "He was just kidding." He tries to put his hand on my neck, but I tighten up my shoulders and arch my back and he pulls it away, slowly.


The skin of the mango is bitter and tough. Technically you can bite through the skin, but it's best to just avoid it completely. Mangoes fall into the same family as poison ivy and poison oak, and for some, mango skin can close up the throat and cover the body with hives. The easiest way to peel a mango is to run a small, sharp paring knife down the sides of the fruit, just under the skin. Underneath that tough layer, the meat of the fruit is soft and juicy. And while the cushion of fibrous, golden orange looks sweet enough to sink your teeth into, it surrounds a hard, oversize pit that often fools the unsuspecting mango eater. If you think you can chop right down the middle, you'll find yourself stopped by this tough, oblong inner core. It's this core that gives the fruit its peculiar shape. The same core serves as a seed for the next mango tree.

When I move to California from the East after college, I see mangoes for the first time in abundance. They come directly from the Philippines, supplying the strong Filipino community that exists south of the Bay Area. For the first time in my life, I have no difficulty finding the oriental stores. On the buses, I am not the only one with black hair or thick dark lips. I have a community of friends who, for the first time, eat what I eat, look like I look. I am tempted to start little romances with the boys in this group, but back away because they look too much like relatives.

I call home all the time to tease my father about the Manila mangoes. "You're right, Dad," I say. "They are the best in the world. I eat them every day. They're so small, I sometimes eat them twice a day."

When I go to the market in Chinatown, I hunch over the vegetable and fruit stands and pick out food I know I've eaten before and liked. Bitter melon. Long beans. I call my mother and ask her how to cook them.

It's a Saturday when I'm at the market scooping tofu from a tall white bucket. There's an overweight, tattooed man standing over the mango crate. He's holding a small Manila mango in his hand, gripping it so tightly that the angel on his forearm looks like she's grimacing. I must be staring at him because when he looks over to my side of the stand, I shift my eyes away quickly and pretend I'm completely involved with the tofu.

"Hey . . . hey!" I hear him yell.

I look over and he's facing me, still holding the mango. He lifts his sunglasses so they sit on his forehead. He smiles at me.

"You know all about these, don't ya honey?" he asks, still smiling, "These here mangoes. This one look good to you?" I'm about to tell him to go for it, to watch out for the bruised one. But before I have time to open my mouth, I notice his eyes rolling down my face, over my chest, and along my backside. I want to see the sweetness in his smile and to hear the polite, innocuous words coming from his mouth. But I can't get over what his eyes have already done. I feel like I've seen that look before and it's saying to me, *Honey, I bagged four or five of you in 'Nam. Yummy.* He is still smiling, waiting for me to answer.

"No," I say instead, with my mother's accent. I smile, close my eyes, bow repeatedly, and tell him, "No, no, me no speak no English. So sowwy." I leave the tofu in the bucket and go running down Grant Street.

I admit to being a sucker for all the mango treats, the artificially flavored mango drinks, the mango hard candy. Dried mango is sometimes considered its own kind of delicacy. It comes in small plastic bags at those oriental food markets. Not quite artificial, not quite the real thing. These mango slices are cut from the real fruit, sugared and dehydrated until they are intensely sweet, like candy. They are addictive, but tough like beef jerky. Enjoying a bite requires you to rip a piece off firmly with your teeth.

The man I live with now has blond curly hair that sticks up in the morning. We are friends from college. After meeting each other again years after graduation, we long-distance phone-dated for a while before we moved to the same city and decided to share a closet-sized apartment. He hates that my long hair clogs up the shower drain, hates that I don't clean it out before I exit the bathroom. He tells me I snore and drool, that all my clothes have stains on the front; I tell him to shove it. I don't sit next to him at dinner parties; I don't hold his hand in the park. My friends ask me if we even like each other. "Ummmmmmmm," I say.

He hates that I don't buy peanut butter, I hate that he doesn't drink Coke. He challenges everything I say. When I protest, he concentrates on my words and reasons, not on the shape of my lips or the breathiness of my voice. We laugh at our height difference, at the opposing shades of our skin. At night, he pulls me over to his side of the bed. He puts his hand on my hip, and rolls me backward toward him. I feel his breath behind my ear, and I like it too much to push him off.

He tells me he thinks that mangoes are best in the morning, that technically, they could replace oranges and bananas as his all-time favorite breakfast fruit.

"All-time?" I ask, laughing at his seriousness.

"The explosion," he says. His hands expose his fleshy white palms and his fingers shoot out in all directions. "Mangoes are going to explode onto the American scene." His smile is devilish, his enthusiasm contagious. "Explode, I say!" He stands, swipes a mango dramatically from the bowl on the table. I'm laughing still, laughing at this conversation so early in the morning.

Before I stop, he has already sat down. He cups the mango gently in his hand, runs a thin, short blade slowly under the reddish yellow skin. He pulls the knife toward his body, something I was taught never to do, but his movement is controlled and slow. I watch the veins in his wrist become more defined against his skin, more blue. Once the inside of the fruit is fully exposed, he cuts off a narrow bright slice. It is slippery between his fingers. He puts it to his thin lips, the nectar of the mango running from the pinched corners of his mouth and down along his chin. He lets the piece sit on his tongue, breathes deeply, and then swallows it whole.

# Urdu, My Love Song

### Rasma Haidri

In a restaurant called Gandhi, a sari-clad woman brings rice to my table and I want to say *shukria*. The word rolls down my tongue, then stops before my dread of being wrong. It is one of the few Urdu words I know, and I think it means "thank you." Or does it mean "please"? On the other hand, *shukria* may have something to do with sugar. I'm unsure. All I know is I learned the word from my father in India during my first visit to his homeland. He most likely explained the word to me in his Dr. S. Zafar Ali Haidri manner of learned professor instructing pupil.

"So you see, honey, the word *shukria*, when pronounced in the Hindi, *shoo-KRI-ah*, in this region of India means 'thank you, kindly.' However, when pronounced in the Urdu of the Punjab as *SHU-kri-ah*, it means most simply 'please.'"

Probably none of this is accurate. At age twenty I was too sure of myself to take notes, so now, twenty years later, I'm too unsure of the meaning of *shukria* to try it out on the waitress.

My confusion around *shukria* and the overlapping meanings of "please" and "thank you" is confounded by the fact that my father used these words differently than anyone else I knew growing up in the South in the 1960s. He was a biochemist, a Fulbright scholar from the Indian Subcontinent whose work in pharmaceutical research had brought us to Oak Ridge, Tennessee, Atomic City U.S.A. True to his image as an upper-class Indian, my father always wore a three-piece suit. To my chagrin, he even attended my Girl Scout father-daughter picnic in this attire, and further embarrassed me by saying "please" (meaning "yes") when offered a slab of Jell-O, and "thank you" (meaning "no, of course not, you filthy infidel!") when someone made the faux pas of offering him a hunk of ham.

We lived in Wiltshire Estates, a settlement of farmettes within the Oak Ridge city limits. Our neighbor Mr. McNabb, in stark contrast to my father, was a true Southerner. The McNabb yard was a mess of tractor tires, odd pieces of metal, and a gaggle of kids and dogs named Mickey, Mackey, Marty, Mitsy, Mindy, and Misery. Mr. McNabb, being neighborly, would lean over our oak-rail fence, remove the chaw-straw from his mouth, and offer, "Howbow summadose toon'p gweens?" I accepted the turnip greens and brought them to my mother, a Wisconsin-born Norwegian, who giggled as I imitated Mr. McNabb's hillbilly talk, and then shoved the greens into the growl of the garbage disposal. She had no idea how to cook them. If my father were around, he would hack them up in a curry and serve them alongside rice and mango chilies. And if he heard me and my brothers mocking Mr. McNabb's vernacular, he would yelp, "Nyaap! Bad manners!" and send us out of the room with a wave of his cuff-linked, manicured hand.

My brothers and I grew up in a linguistic no-man's-land between our well-educated Asian father and our hillbilly neighbor. To us, the word "please" (followed by the obligatory-and-punishable-by-hellfire-if-omitted "ma'am" or "sir") preceded requests such as, "May I have another helping of that bodacious marshmallow salad?" "Thank you (ma'am or sir)" was what we said before stabbing the sticky mess with a fork. Unlike my father or Mr. McNabb, we spoke "normal" English.

My father's English included other oddities, such as "up-a-stairs," which sent us rolling on the floor in convulsions every time we heard it. There were stories from our parents' early years, when my dad thought a baby sitter was a kind of chair they were going to leave one of us in, or that fried chicken wings were called "flies." My father understood the comic value of his lingo and exercised it to the fullest. His regular deadpan reference to my friend Peggy Mead as "Meggy Peed" never failed to send my mother into a fit of red-faced laughter. I didn't laugh. My father's feigned inability to learn my own best friend's name was an annoying reminder that he was different, and therefore the rest of us had to be, too.

My father's outsider language and peculiar accent were just part of his overall eccentricity. It was impossible to figure him out. His formal dress and fasting at Christmas were oddly juxtaposed with his applying his background in physical science to our dog, who had been hit by a car. He set the creature's broken leg with a stick and bandaging tape, and stitched up the wounds with mercerized cotton thread. One afternoon I came home to find him butchering one of our sheep in the storeroom. At times he worked for several drug companies at once and would disappear for months on business to places like New Brunswick and Grosse Pointe Woods, whose very names connoted illusions of grandeur. For the longest time I believed that "Miami" was his "Ami." For the most part, his absences were a welcome reprieve from the intensity of his presence. When he was home, I could be snagged into one of his somnolent lectures on an endless array of scholarly topics, ranging from the history of Islam to the workings of the carburetor engine. I wondered what life was like for kids with normal dads who spoke normal English and, for example, knew something about baseball.

I enjoyed some of my father's quirks. He brought home RC Cola, which no one else seemed to know about. He filled glass jars with a perfect mixture of salty cashews and moist yellow raisins. He could create a delicious meal from whatever he found around the kitchen, and for breakfast he served strong creamy tea and a one-egg omelet folded neatly in the center of my plate like a good-news letter. He told us an Indian folk tale that included a banana leaf SO BIG that his wide arms pushed us helterskelter off the bed. When he sang to us in Urdu, the words themselves were pure music. As much as I was vexed by his English, I was entranced by the exotic and mysterious tones of his native tongue.

When I was nine, the ladies from the Baptist Outreach Mission offered to take us kids to church on Sundays. When they came to the door my mom decided I was of age and offered me up like a little lamb. As an agnostic Lutheran, she reckoned that some religion was better for me than none. And my father, who was away most of the time anyway, knew the Bible Belt provided no Muslim alternative. He was content to let us kids grow up to be regular Christian Americans.

If only it had been that easy.

I sat in the golden oak pew in Robertsville Baptist Church on my first Sunday, rubbing my thumb over a pearly white pin with blue letters that spelled VISITOR. "No thank you, ma'am," I said to the flowery-smelling ladies from the Outreach who asked if I wanted to Go Forward at the Call and Be Saved. I liked being a visitor. I liked my smooth white button with the blue letters. I wasn't at all sure I liked what was going on up front where the preacher was waving his arms and shouting, and people were sobbing into their hands.

Down in the Sunday school classroom, pretty Miss Thomas smiled at us and talked, but I wasn't paying attention to her words. I wondered if she knew there was a color difference between her face and her neck where the makeup ended. I decided that when I grew up I'd rub the makeup all the way down my neck so it wouldn't show. I'd rub it all the way into my blouse. As I stared at Miss Thomas's white pillar neck between her pale lemon suit and black flipped-out hair, I noticed that she was talking about other religions. I raised my hand and said that my father was a Muslim, we were raised like Muslims and didn't eat pork, not even ham at Christmas. Once my mom hid bacon in the freezer because she was a Lutheran, I said, but we had to make sure it was gone before my dad came home so we ate the whole package before his plane landed and I got a headache. And one time our mom gave our dad a leather notepad with his name stamped on it in gold, but he yelled and she cried because on the back it said GENUINE PIGSKIN, and what was she thinking? Our hot dogs were called "beef franks" and our language was Urdu. I could read it and write it, and yes, next Sunday I'd bring some in to show the class.

I left the church sickened by the gravity of my deception. Days passed in fear and dread until I was engulfed in an all-encompassing existential numbness. I spent Saturday afternoon crouched on the carpet slowly fashioning curlicues on a square of paper with a fat lead pencil. This was Urdu. At least this was sort of what Urdu looked like in the exotic books next to the *Physicians' Desk Reference* behind the glass doors of my father's mahogany bookcase.

My father wasn't home that week, but I would not have approached him with my problem if he had been. I had told the Sunday school class that I could read, write, and speak Urdu, and the enormity of the lie made me unable to admit the deception even to myself, not to mention my father. Even pretty Miss Thomas's smile couldn't pierce the wall of self-delusion that insulated me from the fact that my language resembled Mr. McNabb's more than my own father's. The truth was that Urdu, along with banana leaves, elephants, tigers, and the buttery ghee that made Little Black Sambo's pancakes so delicious, was not really part of my life. I wanted it to be, but it wasn't. I was just a skinny brown girl running barefoot in the hills of Tennessee, scooped up by Baptists and dressed in Sunday clothes with a nickel in the palm of my white glove for the collection basket.

Sunday again. I sat stiff and wordless in my pew as the throng sang "Softly and Tenderly Jesus Is Calling!" and the Saved Went Forward at the Call. Instead of a white VISITOR button, I held the piece of Urdu writing I had promised Miss Thomas. Down in the Sunday school classroom I unfolded the small page for all to see. Then, ignoring the look of concern on Miss Thomas's face, I read my Islamic scripture to the class.

"*Nnngha-chokri goo dal!*" I began, imitating the sounds that flowed like song from my father's throat when he talked on the phone to Karachi. "*Chaa-beep hoori gangani? Gung challee lohr reena!*" and so on. I continued for minutes. When I finished, Miss Thomas's eyes were wide open and her skin above the jawline a deeper shade than usual. She cracked out a small "thank you." I sat down and stuffed the paper deep inside my zippered black leather King James Bible.

That's all I remember of Sunday school at Robertsville Baptist Church. I never did go Forward to Be Saved and I must have been a great disappointment to Miss Thomas and the ladies of the Outreach Mission. My disappointment with myself was too grave to register. At home, I ripped up the piece of hateful scribbling, tearing it over and over, driven by confusion, self-loathing, and a fearful panic that someone would find it.

When I was twelve I was introduced to the secrets of the sari. We were in Manhattan, where we often spent summers since my father kept an apartment there for work. A Hindi business associate of his took it upon herself to teach me how to fold, tuck, and drape the long cloth over my still boyish body. Then she gave me a sari to keep. It was yellow chiffon with silver embroidery and had an orange midriff-baring top. All summer I practiced folding the long sheer cloth, and wore the sari over jeans in case of accidental unfurling.

One afternoon my father double-parked the car to run an errand, leaving me in charge of my little brother. I felt important in the driver's seat, traffic grinding past my window. Suddenly my brother opened the back door and started to get out, right into the street. The scene is frozen in my memory: my brother in a striped polo shirt, Beatles haircut, one leg still in the car; me, exiting through the open driver's window, my long brown arm trailing yellow chiffon; the avenue, resounding with Manhattan's symphony—horns, motors, brakes, shouts; and then the clean, clear snap of a newspaper being opened by a man jaywalking toward our car. I noticed the man at the moment I grabbed my brother and started scolding him at the top of my lungs in something resembling primeval screams:

"*Djeepchok kali sin heh nodra! Guldoobi kahan fedrani!*"

As my fake Urdu poured forth, the man looked up from his newspaper and met my eyes. For an instant I wondered if he knew that I was not really a fascinating foreign national speaking an exotic tongue. Did he see the blue jeans under my sari? My brother staggered stunned and pale back into the car, and I opened the door to resume my place in the driver's seat. There was something awful happening here, something deceitful and unbearably pathetic, but I let it go. I tried neither to understand nor explain it. I knew my brother was too little to be able to relate this scene to my father, or worse, to the woman whose yellow sari I wore. I let myself believe that I had pulled it off and that the man with the newspaper had been duly impressed by my exotic dress and speech. He saw that I was no ordinary American. But deep down I knew. I knew that this strange outburst just showed how lost I was, cut off from the land of my birthright and the elusive mysteries of my glorious ancestral tongue.

When I was twenty-one I got married. We gave my parents three days' notice of the wedding. My mother immediately fell to worrying, while my father announced he would make the cake. The night before the wedding, he stayed up baking cakes of descending sizes from whatever we had on hand of assorted mixes. He formed these into a pyramid, which he inscribed with pink Arabic script like the marble detail embedded in the Taj Mahal. I never thanked my father for that cake. We were young, caught up in our ultra-nontraditional wedding, and didn't think we even needed a cake. Now I see it was the most generous gift. How my father must have innovated in our poorly equipped kitchen to make different-sized layers, two colors of frosting, and something with which to write. The inscription was Urdu love poetry or marriage verses from the Koran. He told us, but I don't remember. In one photograph, my husband and I are standing with my parents behind the cake. My mother looks distressed. My father is smiling behind dark sunglasses. There might have been a joke on the order of "Meggy Peed" written on that cake, but only he would have known.

The winter after I got married, I wrote to my father asking about a song he used to sing when we were little. *May-rahah-salam-alay-ajum*. It was, and remains, the most tender memory of my childhood. I missed that song. I longed for it. I asked him to record it for me. Perhaps I could learn it and someday sing it for my own children. At Christmas it arrived: a homemade cassette with "Urdu Wedding Songs" written on it in both Urdu and English. For weeks I played the tape and attempted to sing along, but the bell-like tone of my father singing Urdu was a music my voice could not make. After a while I packed the tape away, worried it would break with wear and I would lose the song forever.

When my daughter was five, her Montessori preschool introduced the children to Indian culture. I suggested she write and tell my father about it. "Ask Nano to teach you the Urdu alphabet," I said. She called him "Nano" instead of "Grandfather," just as at her age I called him "Abba" instead of "Daddy." A short while later her study packet arrived: homemade flash cards of the Urdu alphabet scripted in Arabic with phonetic English renditions and a cassette tape for pronunciation. It was a full-blown Dr. S. Zafar Ali production—each letter was an artistic composition, and the tape included a short history of the etymology of Urdu as well as pronunciation exercises. We admired the cards and listened to my father's sonorous voice on the scratchy tape. But neither my daughter nor I learned the Urdu alphabet.

Each time we moved, I worried about the cards being lost. "Where are those flash cards Nano made you?" I would ask, and my daughter would dutifully produce them. I would take out the cards and examine the letters that still resembled art more than language, then tuck them back into the Chase Manhattan check box my father had sent them in. Having the cards seemed proof that Urdu was still part of my life. Someday my daughter would learn the alphabet. Maybe I would, too. But that conviction was as transparent as the yellow sari I kept carefully wrapped up in a box. Even after visits with my Karachi cousins and traveling across India, *shukria* (meaning "please" or "thank you" or "sugar") and *challo* (meaning "get a move on" to a rickshaw driver) is all the Urdu I know how to say.

I did learn how to write my name. "Rasma" is Latvian, but my father chose the name for its resonance with his language. "So you see, honey, *RAHZ-ma* in Arabic means 'my flower.' However, *Rah-ZI-ma*, in Persian, from which we have derived Urdu, means 'my secret' or 'our secret' in the manner in which you are your mother's and my secret." I even attempted a semester of Urdu in college, but my name remains the one word I know how to write in my father's language. *Rasma*. My secret.

When my father died, his younger brother ordered a Muslim burial. My mother and I knew my father would want to be cremated, but my uncle said this was abhorrent. Without a proper Muslim burial my father's soul would roam the earth disconsolate. *Hindus* were cremated. I wondered if this had been my father's intent, a sly last jab at his brothers whom he loved to provoke with religious arguments. Nonetheless, my mother and I agreed to let the Islamic Center take care of everything.

At the funeral, my mother and my daughter and I were relegated to the women's section. It was a vast room with mirrors covering the length of one wall and not a stick of furniture in it. My uncle had instructed us to wear head scarves. We shuffled around, avoiding ourselves in the mirrors and not daring to speak as rhythmic chanting rose from the men's section on the other side of the wall. I searched in vain for peepholes to get a glimpse of what was going on. When my uncle came in, I asked to see my father's body. He said it was not possible, that women could not enter the prayer hall. When I insisted, he consulted with the mullah, who allowed me to come in for just a moment. I wasn't a Muslim woman anyway.

My father, wrapped in a white shroud, was lying on a straw mat on the floor with all his teeth removed and the blue-ink tattoo on his right bicep clearly visible. It startled me. I hadn't seen that tattoo for years, not since I was little enough to call him Abba. He would lie on the floor in his undershirt, lifting me on his feet to guess my weight. The tattoo had been given to my father by the Royal Indian Army to signify his status as a Muslim. It was the name of God, and to me it looked like a single harmonious letter from the Urdu card pack. I loved that tattoo. I wanted to possess it. A scheme of cutting it out of his arm rushed madly through my head. I longed for that tattoo as much as I had longed for my father's song the first winter of my adulthood. But now I was being ushered out. I looked up over the sea of men bending and bowing over a myriad of small prayer rugs. My brothers looked as helpless as I felt. They couldn't even mouth these prayers for our father. Who were all these strangers? Where was my father's prayer rug and his blue-cloth Koran? How could we save his tattoo? Then, from some recess in my being, or from the air just above my right ear, I heard the peculiar voice that as a child had sometimes made me cringe and sometimes dream of dappled jungle leaves and elephants. "Oh honey," my father said, "it does not matter."

I felt a weight lift from my shoulders. I looked around and saw how, to my father, this could all be quite amusing. His women trying to be demure while fighting off scarves that wanted to slip over our noses; his sons mute and awkward in three-piece suits and sanctified bare feet; himself, our only translator, dead on the floor.

"Oh honey, it does not matter."

It was true. I smiled to myself, and took one last look at the beautiful sky-blue tattoo. This was Urdu. It had come to me, and was leaving, with my father. Its mysterious curves were inextricable from him, indelibly marked on his skin. But all my life I had heard its love song. It didn't matter that it could never be mine.

# HELLO KITTY PACKS HEAT

## Tina Lee

I HAVE A WHITEBOARD BY MY DESK at work where I keep a list of the most pressing issues in need of resolution. To keep myself focused and motivated, I use double underlines, asterisks, all caps, and exclamation points liberally. One morning I arrived at work to find that one of my coworkers had drawn a picture next to one of my most menacing listings about a group that owed me a critical deliverable. It featured Hello Kitty, drawn in blue erasable marker, wearing a short minidress that showed off her squat legs; her head was cocked innocently to one side, she had a bow in her hair, and she was cradling a very large automatic weapon between her chubby little arms.

At first I was taken aback. The illustration was hysterical, but wrong. And the fact that this subversive act was committed by a white male made it that much more perverse. Hello Kitty, after all, is the iconic Asian equivalent of America's Minnie Mouse, loved by millions around the world, across all racial and socioeconomic boundaries. Nonthreatening and noncontroversial, with a penchant for all things pink and plastic, Hello Kitty is the epitome of "cute" and "nice." As the cartoon ambassador of Asian kitsch, her adorable face adorns pencil boxes, mini desktop trashcans, travel mugs, alarm clocks, lunch boxes, mouse pads, hair clips, cell-phone charms, shower caps, and expandable suitcases with wheels. Hello Kitty elicits childlike glee in me, which is exactly why I found the sketch of her on my whiteboard holding a machine gun particularly blasphemous. The more I looked at it, however, the more I came to realize how astute my coworker was. *I am Hello Kitty with a machine gun—except way scarier, because I have a mouth.* No wonder boys are afraid of me.

In all honesty, I have never been the quiet, demure Asian lotus flower of which male fantasies are made. As the first-generation American-born daughter of Chinese immigrants who divorced when I was only four years old, my upbringing was anything but fantastic. My father was a physically and verbally abusive gambling addict, and shortly after the divorce, my mother fled with my younger brother and me to my maternal grandmother's house in Hong Kong. Unfortunately, what we found there was equally unsavory. Armed with only a high school education, my mother could not find gainful employment that afforded her the luxury of childcare. Furthermore, having kids from a failed marriage also made her "damaged goods" in the Hong Kong dating market, so she left us in my grandmother's hands. My grandmother shared my father's physically and verbally abusive nature, and my brother and I put up with it for an entire year before spilling the beans. Even then my mother didn't do much to set things right, and we remained in Hong

Kong for a little over three years, ultimately returning to America when my mother remarried. We became her "dirty little secrets" who technically did not exist, and so she sent us back to live with our father, thereby affording me the opportunity of spending my formative years as a semi-orphaned fat girl who learned to use intelligence and humor to mask emotional vulnerability.

My paternal grandmother, who immigrated to the United States in the 1970s, right before I was born, took over the most basic of parental duties. She and my grandfather lived in a two-room apartment in San Francisco's Chinatown that was only a ten-minute bus ride from the apartment my brother and I shared with our father. On weekdays during the times between regular school and Chinese school, and then between Chinese school and our commute home, my grandmother worked as hard to feed us as she did to excite our fears. Over countless meals with dishes such as pig brain soup, salted dried fish, Chinese sausage, steamed pork with pickled cabbage, and boiled iceberg lettuce with oyster sauce, my grandmother taught us that African American people are violent and stupid, that homeless people are lazy, and that we must eat every grain of rice in our bowl if we wanted to marry a spouse with flawless skin. Through her eyes, we also learned that the world is not a safe place, and because scarcity abounds and disasters loom, one must save everything all the time. To this end, my grandmother hoarded an impressive supply of pink plastic grocery bags, napkins and pilfered sugar packets from the McDonald's down the block, and Chinese red envelopes that had once held cash gifts from family and friends that she'd reuse for her own gift-giving occasions, as well as a large inventory of government-issued boxed and canned goods that she didn't know how to cook because the labels were in English.

On weekends my brother and I played hide-and-seek at the sweatshop where my grandmother worked. Sometimes we helped out with the sewing. Oftentimes my grandmother stayed to play mah-jongg with her coworkers late into the night while we engaged in general naughtiness in the alleyway outside, where one could never quite distinguish between rats and cats. I suspect it was around this time that I picked up my grandmother's obsessive-compulsive tendencies.

My paternal grandfather was only marginally involved. He'd show up with treats once in a while, whenever he was able to tear himself away from his mah-jongg and horse-racing buddies at the Lee's Family Association. He also worked the late shift as a janitor in an office building in downtown San Francisco, so he never ate evening meals with us. Every weekday he'd leave for work right around 4:00 PM with a brown paper bag containing his dinner, right before my brother and I would leave for Chinese school. Since my grandparents don't eat sandwiches, I'm still unsure as to what the contents of that brown paper bag were. It was during these preteen years that I learned to use sarcasm and became acquainted with the effects of racism, sexism, and social inequity, though at the time I did not know their names.

My father's shortcomings created quite a harrowing teenage experience for me. As if adolescence were not hard enough, mine included sporadic meetings at mortgage-lending institutions where I served as my grandparents' translator as banking officers explained why they were going into foreclosure on our house whenever my father fell behind on loan payments. My brother and I also struggled with mismatched-food quandaries, often grappling with such culinary puzzles as having cereal but no milk, bread but no deli meat, rice but no main dishes with which to eat it. Commuting an hour and a half every day from my house to a college-preparatory geek high school wearing a cheerleading uniform through one of the worst ghettoes in San Francisco forced me to grow an inner strength, as did a particularly brutal beating from my father one fateful night when I not only managed to shed no tears, but valiantly looked him in the eyes at the end and informed him calmly that that would be the last time.

No doubt, that was when I became Hello Kitty with a mouth.

Lessons in the value of proper planning began shortly thereafter as I began to plot my escape. I knew how much money I needed for rent and food even before I knew which college I wanted to attend. And when I fell in love with a beautiful half white, half African American boy at age nineteen, I seized the opportunity to move into the apartment he shared with his HIV-infected, ex-heroin-addict mother. This I did against my paternal grandparents' wishes, of course, while working at a law office and attending the City College of San Francisco, both part-time.

Abuse, treachery, addiction, disease; racial, cultural, and generational discord—my life is so *The Joy Luck Club* meets Jerry Springer on acid. Such trauma exacerbated an affliction I was already prone to due to my heritage, the "Angry but Mute Martyr's Disease," and it took a potent combination of spending three years at a women's college and four years of weekly behavioral-therapy sessions with a licensed clinical social worker to overcome it. For all intents and purposes, these experiences, which have left indelible marks on my psychic screen, are indeed quite extraordinary when put in a Chinese American context. After all, divorce in the Chinese American community is rare. Deadbeat dads, as well as mothers who abandon their children, are rare. And daughters who raise themselves to become relatively well-adjusted corporate cogs with MBAs are rarer still. My personal history has shaped my frame of reference. Therefore, I don't credit docility with helping me develop from the person I was into the person I am.

So one would not need much imagination to see how my sensibilities can give rise to a plethora of problems when dating within a hegemonic patriarchal paradigm. Take, for example, the case of David, an old childhood friend. He's the youngest of nine children, and his sister-in-law, Aunt Susan, has been friends with my mother since we were children. David and I apparently attended both elementary and high school together, but I don't remember him from elementary school and he hardly ever spoke to me in high school. David and I ran into each other on a busy street in downtown San Francisco during lunchtime one day. We exchanged contact information and then made tentative plans over email to meet for lunch. But before any such plans could be confirmed, David stopped responding to my emails. There's nothing I detest more than bad follow-through. In a world with text messaging, instant messaging, emails, voice mails, and faxes, where we're all less than six degrees away from Kevin Bacon, a bad follow-through is absolutely inexcusable. Thus, I found it entirely appropriate to torture him when he showed up for a family Thanksgiving dinner not long afterward.

First, I publicly showered him with pleasantries, throwing him a big, tight hug in front of everyone—it was wholly sincere, if a bit over-the-top. Then, when he went to fetch his food, I swapped his regular folding chair for one covered with a Hello Kitty chair protector. Unbeknownst to him, he gaily sat in it all through dinner. More harmless fun was had over the course of the evening, and, by the end, we had successfully worked past his transgression and I was able to bid farewell to an old friend with peace in my heart.

Aunt Susan, however, did not share my sense of contentment. Before I left, she said, "You know, Tina, you've scared David. He's very shy. Chinese boys like quieter and gentler girls, so if you want a Chinese boyfriend, you're going to have to tone it down. You have to at least *pretend* to be docile and let them think they're in control until you get them." I can honestly say that had she not been the hostess, and had I not been socialized with silly notions about familial piety and respect for elders that prevented me from entangling myself in an all-out catfight on the front lawn while her husband hosed us down, someone would have had to have held my weave, my earrings, and my nails that night because I would have gone Ghetto Kitty on her ass. Whether it was what that social situation required or Aunt Susan's own inclination to occupy the far-right region of the docility continuum (at least when males are involved), suddenly, a woman who had been only peripherally involved in my life felt compelled to announce in public that I needed a lesson or two in the art of deception to hook a man—even one I had no romantic interest in to begin with. I believe some justice could have been had if someone would have pulled David aside and schooled him on the finer points of how to hook a girl. Tip number one: Always observe decorum by conducting a proper follow-through after each social interaction that requires some form of reciprocation. Tip number two (and this point is most essential): Stop. Being. A. Fucking. Pussy.

There are five things that I have an extreme aversion to: panty lines; whiners who don't take responsibility for their own actions; closed-minded, inflexible cretins who impede progress; passive-aggressives who lack moral courage; and the faint-hearted who infect the world with their fear. Given my gestalt, it should be no surprise that I value initiative, assertiveness, and self-reliance, and appreciate equity and cognitive complexity. After all that's happened to me, or maybe even because of it, I am a fantastic cheerleader who approaches life with vivacity and measures my time by opportunity cost. I also believe I have the power and the responsibility to create meaningful social change. Yet I find it ironic that the very same attributes that would make a white male seem highly desirable when profiled on match.com are considered liabilities to be mitigated when they belong to a Hello Kitty. "Watch out! She's cute but dangerous! And don't ever get on her bad side!"

"I feel competitive toward you," confessed one hunky Asian Boy Scout who's now engaged to an antithetical version of me. "You see, in every relationship there must be a flower and a gardener, and unfortunately, we're both flowers." I, too, later came to realize why our relationship would never work, though my conclusion resulted from an entirely different set of assumptions and reasoning. Yes, it may not be logistically feasible for both people in a romantic relationship (or any relationship for that matter) to be flowers at the same time; however, I believe these roles can be interchangeable if both partners are committed to the relationship and approach each other with open-mindedness and flexibility. This requires maturity, empathy, confidence, and self-awareness, however; and between biology, overbearing Chinese mothers who coddle their sons, and the emasculation of Asian American men on a societal level, I fear many of my Chinese American brothers won't evolve to this stratum of emotional intelligence until I have "rocks-in-socks" boobs in my shoes and a once ghetto-fabulous booty hitting the backs of my knees.

"Just stop going there, Tina. Asian boys are not for you," my very un-Chinese-male brother says to me all the time. "Let's face it. You're going to end up with a white guy." Although this is a distinct possibility given the demographics of my immediate surroundings and my proclivities, I feel uneasy about accepting this statistical probability as fate. After all, I'm only a stone's throw away from the Chinatown where I grew up, and few white males will ever be able to fully understand, let alone appreciate, who I am and why I am. I still feel pangs of guilt whenever I visit the Vietnamese nail shop where I get my bimonthly manicures and pedicures, and the thought of bringing my dirty laundry to the Chinese dry cleaner in my neighborhood is absolutely inconceivable in spite of my workaholic schedule.

As a socially mobile, first-generation Asian American female, I remain painfully aware of what it means to be "Chinese" and "Chinese female." I know the history, I understand the diasporas, and I am well-versed in the socioeconomics. Therefore, I feel the guilt, the obligation, and the need to hold on to my cultural heritage as gender roles and race relations are continually renegotiated in American society.

So often, I find myself overcompensating for all of this. While I follow all traffic rules diligently when driving, signaling at every turn and always coming to a complete stop at each intersection with a stop sign, I grow louder whenever there's a demure Asian female in the room. Overeducated and psychoanalyzed, I opine my over-the-top, anti-racist and anticlassist feminist views with a vocabulary and a voice that my mother and grandmother don't have. I have an obligation to "represent," especially in corporate or political situations where I may not be expected to do so. This is my responsibility as a survivor, and survivors are just overly sensitive and defiantly cocky like that.

"You're not *that* scary," said one very clever male friend. "You just seem scary because the reality of who you are is so vastly different from who you're supposed to be. In fact, if you were a white male, you wouldn't be scary at all." Oh, how true! If I were a white male, I'm absolutely certain I'd be a gigolo swimmin' in honeys, pimpin' hos in different area codes. But alas, I am a first-generation Chinese American female who was raised by a traditional, neurotic grandmother with a history of "Angry but Mute Martyr's Disease." And though I'm fairly adept at traversing the diametrically opposed boundaries of my biculturalism most of the time, I find myself constrained by some very traditional Chinese ideals when it comes to men. In spite of the liberal views I espouse about feminism, my views on sexual experimentation remain erudite and theoretical. For example, inspired by too many episodes of *Sex in the City*, there was a time in my recent past when I tried dating multiple men at once. Copious data points, I decided, were what I needed to develop a sound hypothesis demystifying the opposite sex. Much to my chagrin, that exercise proved too complicated and cumbersome in my ADHD-addled, time-constrained world, and led only to more undue confusion.

I felt tremendous guilt whenever I inadvertently called one by the wrong name or made reference to a conversation I'd had with someone else. I snuck off to the bathroom during dinner with one to send text messages to another. Like appointments and errands, I scheduled dates based on geographic proximity and whether the nature of the encounter made it efficient to do so. With a divided heart, I was driven to commit these horrible acts of disloyalty that would no doubt bring shame upon my family if ever disclosed. And if merely dating more than one man at once can bring on such feelings of shame and confusion, I'd surely buckle under the cognitive dissonance that would result if I ever had sexual relations with more than one partner at a time. In fact, I've found that I can't even handle one-night stands because I have that common perennial "girl problem"—I equate sex with love.

Too Chinese to be a wanton sex goddess yet too American to be a listless martyr, I end up a compulsive serial monogamist with attitude, vacillating between the roles of spontaneous, exuberant lover and overly doting mom; compliant corporate whore and audacious grassroots activist; diplomatic cultural ambassador and nonconformist, feminist commando spy; sometimes-unwitting beauty and often much-too-deliberate brain. Like a chameleon, I adapt my colors to an ever-changing environment because my perception of the world is filtered through three lenses: one Chinese, one American, one female. It's like being a Toyota-esque automobile designed by Chinese engineers specifically to meet American needs, assembled by small-town autoworkers in the heartland adhering to an East/West hybrid set of manufacturing standards, and then marketed to the American consumer as something smart and efficient that'll "love you long time." The complexity involved makes tinkering with any of these interdependent parts a challenging endeavor.

But just as there are mechanically enhanced Toyotas turned into brightly colored rice-rockets, souped up for car shows and street races, there are also Hello Kitties that come with special accessories. While I do indeed have a machine gun and a mouth, I also come with a few diplomas, a spine, a 401(k) plan, and a heart that listens and sings. I'm certain there's a group of Hello Kitty connoisseurs out there who will truly appreciate that.

# PALINDROME

## Lisa Swanstrom

"A man, a plan, a canal: Panama"

LORENZA NUÑEZ, MY MATERNAL great-grandmother, was a witch. Just shy of five feet tall, she was close to eye level with the palms she read, and could trace the design of an entire life in the creases of an open hand.

Her daughter (my grandmother), Margarita Gomez, is a religious fundamentalist. A petite but effective conduit for the righteous wrath of God, she became a *testigo de Jehovah* (Jehovah's Witness) in the 1940s, when she married my grandfather. Even today, at eighty, she will rap forcefully on the doors of strangers, demanding they be saved.

My mother, Madeleine Swanstrom, is half witch, half religious fundamentalist, and sees no contradiction between the two. Get a few drinks in her, and she will alternately quote the vengeful scripture of the God of Abraham and hex the neighbor's dog for whizzing on her front lawn in the suburban town of Thousand Oaks, California, where she now lives.

Of the three worldviews that I have inherited from my mother, grandmother, and great-grandmother, I find my mother's eclectic and contradictory religion—her pick and choose approach to spirituality—the most puzzling. She has no consistency. One day it's "Jesus Saves," and the next it's voodoo dolls and the evil eye. You can't have it both ways.

I like to tell myself that I believe in nothing. But despite my strong claims to materialism, I have on my mantel a fat, golden Buddha, a petite teakwood Buddha, a Jesus-on-wheels action figure, prayer beads, joss candles, and yellow tissue paper to burn for the dead.

I would like to say that this is a collection of kitsch. These items are, after all, tacky and glittery, tawdry as ten-dollar whores. But I bristle at this comparison even as I write it, because I have started to care for them. I dust the golden Buddha before leaving for school each day, and make sure the teakwood Buddha faces the sunlight. There is nothing I have read that suggests that teakwood Buddhas require sunlight—his holiness Siddhartha Gautama is not a fern—but something about his wide smile makes me want to put him in a sunbeam and make that smile grow wider. I keep my prayer beads clean and take Jesus-on-wheels out for a spin when he feels closed in. I light the joss candles when I am feeling blue, feeling grim. And burning yellow tissue paper has helped me get through the death of two close friends.

But I would never tell any of this to my mother.

She would use it as a chisel or a wedge, and wouldn't stop hammering at me until I confessed that I believed in something. And I would, just to get her to leave me alone, when in fact I believe in nothing, and never have.

"You have to believe in something," she says.

I shake my head and shrug.


Because of our religious differences, my mother and I haven't spoken in weeks—not since our argument about Darwin's "theories." This argument started when my mother took a blue marker to an article I'd read about evolution and highlighted every occurrence of the words "possibly," "maybe," "perhaps," "thinks," and "believes" in order to prove how shifty the ground was upon which this whole "monkey science" was based. After this demonstration, I was called to defend, all by myself, one hundred and fifty years of evolutionary biology.

"Explain consciousness," she said.

"It's an accident of—"

"Explain love."

"Sexual selec—"

"Explain why we have more ribs than your father."

"Oh Christ," I said.

"Exactly."

I became exasperated. "It's the twenty-first century we're living in here," I said. "How can you still think that way?"

She clammed up and gave me a look. I held my ground, even as the look grew darker and her lower jaw set, her chin pushed forward, and her lips pressed together, zippered shut.

"How?"

She exhaled a thin, pissed-off whistle. "If you knew where I was raised—how I was raised—how my mother and her mother before her were raised—maybe you would understand how I 'think that way.'" She held up her fingers and made sarcastic quotation marks with them.

I rolled my eyes and threw up my hands. Before leaving, I said that word that all mothers hate to hear: "Whatever."

But she had a point.

Lorenza, Margarita, and my mother, Madeleine, were born and

raised in the Republic of Panama, that narrow isthmus that connects two continents, as well as two oceans, two worlds, two lives: North America to South America, the New World to the Old, my mother's life to mine.

I have never been there. My knowledge of Panama comes to me mediated through old photographs and postcards, faded gourds and bright *molas*. The *molas*, in particular, have always fascinated me. These multilayered collages of fabric are hand stitched by Panama's Kuna Indians, and each *mola* tells a story, in cloth, of Panama: its jungles, its animals, its thick green rivers. It seems to me a strange and exotic place, remote and unknown. I feel no connection to it, for although I am 25 percent Panamanian, in appearance I favor my father, who is a Swede.

My father and I are as white as marshmallows: We burn easily, and insects love us. We belong in Minnesota, with Swedes and Norwegians as deficient in melanin as we are. We certainly don't belong in the jungle. But my mother, who is half Panamanian and half Norwegian—with her black hair, brown eyes, and smooth skin that never wrinkles, even though she is fifty-five—does. She lived the first twenty years of her life in and out of the Canal Zone, collecting seashells at low tide and sipping chilled coconut juice, right from the *pipa*, in her home in Cocolí.

Thinking things over, I feel wistful about how little I know of this period of my mother's life. And I feel ashamed. I cannot stand feeling ashamed, and make up my mind to do something about this rift that has come between us and grown over the years. The idea comes to me on the edge of sleep, in the middle of the night, in a dream of hot green spaces. Why not? I know some Spanish. I have family down there. I have a credit card. Why not? I ask myself again.

The next day I do the legwork. If I fly red-eye and eat cheaply, I can stitch together an itinerary that won't *entirely* break my budget. So, after madly scrambling for cash and begging for an extension of my Citibank credit limit, after sorting out my monthly bills and making hasty arrangements for pet care, I am traveling to Panama to see if I can figure out, after all these years, where my mother is coming from.

My aunt Bibi picks me up at the Panama airport. Even though she has dyed her dark hair blond, I recognize her immediately. Her resemblance to my mother is striking. They are sisters, after all, although the two of them haven't had a civilized conversation in years.

I was, in fact, amazed and touched when my mother showed me the email she had written to her sister about my coming to Panama:

"You know how Lisa is. KEEP HER SAFE . . . Madeleine."

I chose to ignore the first sentence and focus on the second.

"Wow," I said to my mom. "I can't believe you and Bibi are talking again."

"We're not talking," my mother said. "We're emailing. There's a difference."

"You're communicating," I insisted.

She "humphed" at me as I packed.

"Whatever happened with you two?" I asked. "You used to be so close."

She gave me a look from her arsenal of looks. "Don't lend her any money."

Bibi towers over the rest of the people in the waiting area of the airport, and her smile stretches ear to ear, bright red and Carmen Miranda wide. We hug, and all the Spanish I have been practicing comes out in halting sentences, jumbled and twisting. It's not that I have to use Spanish—like my mother, all my aunts and uncles are bilingual—but I want to. I need to, because I am trying to learn to speak my mother's language.

Bibi and I drag my duffel bag, which Bibi immediately nicknames El Muerto, the corpse, out to her old red Tercel. Although she asks me to call her Elizabeth, which is her real name, she is still Aunt Bibi to me. And I am her *tocaya*—her namesake, since Elizabeth, which means

"God has sworn" in Hebrew, is my real name as well, and Lisa is just a diminutive derived from the way Elizabeth sounds in Spanish ("A-lisa-bet").

Bibi's apartment in the banking district is lofty and sprawling, with pale orange tile floors and lots of open space, including one big bedroom, one tiny bedroom that was the maid's quarters in earlier days, a large laundry room, and a veranda. Aunt Bibi is an iridologist and herbalist, a modern-day Panamanian *curandera* who heals with herbs and eye charts, and her boyfriend, José, does massage therapy, so there is also a therapy room and waiting area for their clients.

Once we drop off El Muerto in the small side room that will be my bedroom, Bibi and I sit down in her kitchen and drink hot tea. She looks into my eyes and recommends a lengthy prescription of goldenseal, dong quai, and cascara sagrada. When I tell her that I have no money with which to buy her herbs, she looks disappointed but doesn't press. After an hour of bringing each other up-to-date, Bibi looks at me firmly and says, "How's Mimi? How's my sister?"

I am unsure how to begin. "We fight all the time," I say.

"What do you fight about?"

I tell Bibi about the Darwin article.

"Well," she sips her tea. "I hope you don't believe in *that* nonsense."

"Wait a minute here." I switch back to English. "You don't believe in evolution?"

"*Para nada.*" Her hands fly out definitively. "I'm not related to any monkey."

"But you're not a Christian?"

Bibi sits back in her chair and regards me as one might regard an alien species who has crash-landed on her lawn in the predawn light—rubbing her eyes at this astonishing sight and asking herself, *Am I dreaming?*

"Of *course* I'm a Christian," she says.

"But you believe that herbs can heal and that my eyes reveal what's wrong with me?"

"Absolutely."

"But isn't that like witchcraft?"

Bibi looks at me sideways.

"Am I alone here? Is this a Panamanian thing?"

She shakes her head. "I have someone I want you to meet."

Bibi and I get back into the car and drive to her friend Elisabeth's house, which is not a house, but a garage with a cement floor, on a small side street. Elisabeth, a sixty-year-old woman without a wrinkle in her skin, opens the garage door and says *"Aunque mi casa sea pobre estás bienvenida aquí."* ("Although my house is poor, you are welcome here.") *"Soy Elisabeth."*

We are now three generations of Elizabeths in one room. I won-der superstitiously if this carries any import and make a mental note to look this up in my book of superstition when I get back home.

Elisa is Cuban and makes a mean *ropa vieja*, a stewed and rope-like beef. After eating, we have an extended conversation about the powers of voodoo, which Elisa has (*"gracias a Dios,"* she says—"thank God") left behind. She tells of an evil babalao, a voodoo priest who made cloth dolls and cement saint dolls, and who specialized in the bloodletting of goats and doves.

She speaks quickly, omitting the usual hard r's, so Bibi has to translate:

"I had a saint doll once, and it gave me nothing but trouble. I had one made in my image and it started to fall apart when I came here to Panama, so I rolled it up and made a little place for it inside my suit-case. But when I got here, do you know what happened? The rats ate it. They had a feast! And I threw that saint doll away because I realized then that there is only one true God and his son Jesus Christ."

Bibi nods solemnly after translating this statement and adds, "That sort of voodoo belief system is a form of slavery. It's so incredible that people believe in it today."

Elisa clears the table and brushes me aside, in mock outrage, when I try to help. I am the guest, she insists, and I will do nothing but eat. Once the table is cleared, Elisa dims the lights, and my aunt Bibi pulls out a golden pendulum on a heavy gold chain.

"What's that for?" I ask.

"*Cállate*," Bibi murmurs. I shut up and watch.

Bibi whispers above the chain. All I can make out is "*Cuanto tiempo . . . cuanto tiempo . . .*" ("How long, how long . . .") The rest is too fast for me to follow. The room grows cold, and the hairs on my forearm rise. The pendant sways, swings four times in a circle, and then slows and hangs straight.

Bibi closes her eyes. "*Cuatro meses.*" ("Four months.")

Elisa's eyes shine over. She grabs her apron in her fist and squeezes.

Afterward, we thank her for lunch and leave.

Back in the sunlight, I watch the goose bumps on my arm retreat. I grab Bibi by the elbow. "What the *hell* was *that?*"

Bibi shakes me off gently as we climb into her car and explains that Elisa was asking how long she and her husband would have to wait before they would be able to join the rest of their family in Florida.

"Asking who?" I say. "Who were you asking?"

Bibi shrugs and smiles. "God."


That night Bibi and I stop at a small convenience store, Bodega mi Amiga, and buy a pint of ceviche and a case of Imperial, a Panamanian beer, and sit on her veranda, watching the storm clouds roll in. The ceviche is good—the beer is essential. I slug down a bottle without blinking and devote myself to spreading the ceviche on a cracker. Bibi sips slowly, content, and regards me fondly.

"What did you think of Elisa?"

I hiccup. "She seems nice."

We are quiet for a moment, before I ask: "You don't see a contradiction?"

"What do you mean?"

"Between your faith in God and witchcraft. Between Elisa's faith in God and witchcraft?"

She holds up her index finger. "There is only one true God."

I sigh and shake my head. I think about Elisa's brush with the Babalao and start laughing.

"You know," I say to Bibi, "I thought Babalao was the name of Ricky Ricardo's club on *I Love Lucy*."

"That was Babalu." She laughs, too, and throws a cracker at my head. "Go to bed."


As I lie in bed I think of La Tulivieja, the ash eater.

When I was little my mother terrified me with stories of this old witch who lurked at the river's edge and stole children, carved them up with her long ragged claws, then burned them up and ate their ashes on the sandbank. These are the bedtime stories I grew up with—followed by a prim "say your prayers" before lights out. No wonder I needed a night light until I was sixteen.

Here, now, in Bibi's apartment in Panama, with the storm winds blowing the hanging laundry outside my bedroom so the shirtsleeves dance like the arms of ghosts, I turn the bathroom light on, even though I am twenty-seven years old, and tell myself that I don't believe in anything.

I sleep fitfully, dreaming of golden pendants, voodoo priests, and Ricky Ricardo yelling "Baba-lao!" in a roofless nightclub, as ash rains down on his stage.


The next morning Bibi and I begin our drive north, through the provinces of Panama, Veraguas, Coclé, and Herrera to Chiriquí, where my grandmother Margarita is from.

It will take us seven hours to get to Davíd, so we stop in Santiago and have a full meal of pork chops and *patacones*. Since I arrived in

Panama yesterday, I have felt awkward, conspicuous, and out of place. Eating the *patacones*, however, is like coming home. My mother makes them for me every year on my birthday, if she can find green plantains to squash flat and fry, and it's nice to eat them and not have to explain to anyone what they are.

After lunch we drive through rainstorms in Bibi's old Tercel. As a lightning bolt strikes, illuminating her face, Bibi turns to me and says, "You really don't believe in God?"

I nod, holding on to the armrest of the Tercel as the lightning snakes down. "You really do?"

Bibi nods firmly. "Yes. I believe that I am on this earth for a *purpose*— that I was created by a loving God who has *plans* for me."

I snort. "You sound like Grandma." We both know this is not a compliment. My earliest memory of my grandmother involves her in her house in Florida telling me about Armageddon—before whacking me with her *chancleta* for eating too many cookies. *Chancleta*, which means slipper, was in fact the first word I learned in Spanish, because my grandmother was always whacking—or threatening to whack—with it.

"Do you know anything about your grandmother?" Bibi asks. "My mother."

I snort again. "She has a wicked forehand."

The raindrops smear on the windshield, giving the car a darkly luminous glow. Bibi sighs sadly, taps her hands on the steering wheel, and begins to tell me about Margarita Gomez.


My grandmother was born in a volcanic crater in the province of Chiriquí, Panama, in 1922.

She and her mother, Lorenza, lived near the Chiriquí River, in the dense mountain jungle, and Margarita, whose name means Daisy, remembers how Lorenza sent her out to fetch water from the river when she was four years old. As she bent over the water, she saw jaguar footprints in the mud at the river's edge. After that, she was afraid of being mauled every time she stepped outside.

Margarita never knew her father, Juan Gomez. One day when she was still an infant, he went out hunting and never came back, and she and Lorenza never knew for sure if he was dead or had just abandoned them.

As Margarita grew older, she and Lorenza looked more like nesting doll sisters than mother and daughter. They were both petite and well rounded, with skinny legs, flat feet, and big, soft bosoms. They had the same black hair and intense black eyes; they wore the same clothes; and they lived in the same small house with its dirt floor, tin roof, and thin walls.

When Margarita was thirteen, Lorenza, desperate for money, sold her into marriage to a man named Rafael.

He beat her. He raped her. And, after she had borne a son to him at the age of fourteen, she fled with the baby back to Lorenza in Volcán.

She stayed with Lorenza and found work as a maid and cook at the home of a wealthy lawyer in the nearby town of Davíd. She worked there until she met the man who would, as they say in the breathless manner of soap operas and romance novels, change her life forever.

My grandfather came from North Dakota to Colombia in the 1930s to work for the United Fruit Company. He was a civil engineer; he managed sewage lines and drainpipes and designed garbage sluices for a living. He was tall and lean and spoke schoolbook Spanish with a clean, neat accent. After some time he was transferred to Panama, which wasn't so much of a transfer as it was a change of name, since Panama was part of Colombia before the United States "liberated" it in 1905.

One hot day my grandfather saw Margarita kneading bread outside in the Chiriquí summer. His pulse quickened beneath the pressed lapels of his linen suit. He approached her and said in Spanish, "I would like to taste some of that bread."

They were married shortly afterward. She was eighteen; he was thirty-five. It was his first marriage and her second. The Catholic Church refused to recognize their marriage, since she was still legally married to Rafael. Rafael took her son, because the law and the Church favored the father in such cases. The Church never did recognize her marriage, and Margarita had nothing more to do with papists. She became a Jehovah's Witness soon after.

I am beginning to understand why.

Bibi and I arrive in Davíd and stay at the Hotel Puerta del Sol. The rooms are clean, with high, firm narrow beds, yellow bedspreads, white walls, and cherrywood doors. After a light dinner in the hotel restaurant, we fall asleep early, listening to the rainfall against the window panes.

The next morning we drive around Davíd and Volcán, looking at the coffee farms that line the green mountains. It rains, and the sky looks like a flat gray screen. Lightning bolts strike, the sky flashes, and the earth shakes beneath our car.

We drive to the Chiriquí River and hike above the churning water. I wonder which part of this river's mud held the footprints of the jaguar that frightened my grandmother so, but I'll never know, because Bibi tells me that Lorenza's house is long gone.

As we leave the mountains I fight sleep. "Why did they leave?" I ask, yawning. "When did they move?"

"Papa got a job working for the Canal Zone," Bibi says. "He was a civil servant. He and your Grandpa Swanstrom worked together in the same office."

I shake my head. "That must have been something."

"It was." Bibi laughs. "They didn't get along too well. We'll go to the Canal Zone tomorrow, if you like. I'll show you where they worked. Where your mom and dad went to high school. Where they fell in love."

I would like that. I tell her so, before I fall asleep.

The Canal Zone is a ghost town. What were once the neighborhoods of Cocolí and Rodman are now nothing more than a group of empty houses in extreme disrepair, sagging above cement blocks where neighborhoods once stood. Empty.

Yet in a way, the emptiness of the zone makes it easier for me to imagine my parents being here in the 1960s—my mom in her high heels and knee-length skirt, walking to the Kingdom Hall on Sundays; my dad playing football on the empty field behind Balboa High; Grandpa Swanstrom saving his pennies to go back to Minnesota with my grandmother Anne; my grandfather Berg cutting his own way through the saw grass with a machete to make a shortcut to his house on Nicobar Lane; my grandmother grinding corn and talking endlessly about the Lord.

And the Cocolí pool.

"Your parents' whole romance took place at that pool," Bibi says, and I can see why. Like all pools, it is bright, aqua-blue, clear, and cool. But the heat here is something, way hotter and more humid than Florida, where I was born, and I can see how that pool would have been like paradise during this kind of weather.

I imagine my dad sitting on the lifeguard chair, a stripe of zinc down his nose, my mom climbing out of the water, him seeing her, her seeing him.

An armed guard on a bicycle interrupts my thoughts. We aren't supposed to be in here, poking around. The whole area is under the jurisdiction of the ARI (Autoridad de la Region Interoceanica), which took charge of the redistribution of land after 2000.

The armed guard stops his bike, adjusts his gun. He speaks into his walkie-talkie and looks at us suspiciously.

"There used to be a swing set, playgrounds, and a movie theater when I was a girl," Bibi explains to the guard in Spanish.

He says, "There's nothing here now but mosquitoes."

Bibi remarks how the tables have turned—how it used to be the Panamanians who couldn't come into the zone, and now it's the Panamanians keeping everyone out. The guard smiles and lets us go.

Bibi smiles back, turns to me, and says, "Let's go see the canal."

It says in the museum that the Panama Canal is the "seventh wonder of the industrial world." It's not far-fetched.

The canal is fifty miles long, a green-chambered river surrounded by jungle.

"A man, a plan, a canal—Panama," Bibi says. "It's a palindrome."

"That's my mom's favorite."

Mine is "Satan, oscillate my metallic sonatas," but I decide not to share that with Bibi.

I smile to myself, thinking of the time my mother confiscated my homemade Ouija board and burned it right in front of me, and I realize, taking in the canal—the wall of jungle surrounding it, the dizzy green smell of it, and the waters of two oceans flowing through it—that I have never understood my mother.

Or my grandmother.

I admit to a certain fascination with Lorenza, the witch, but that hardly counts as understanding.

But talking with my aunt Bibi is helping me to come to terms with it all.

We leave the locks when Bibi looks at her watch. "C'mon. We need to go before it closes."

"What?"

"The cemetery."

The Jardín de Paz is huge, sprawling, and unmarked except for a few clay disks not much larger than silver dollars.

Lorenza Nuñez, my great-grandmother, is buried here.

Many of the graves are unmarked except for an even smaller clay disk that says only the grid coordinates of the burial point (G7, for example). But Lorenza has a real tombstone, right next to her recently deceased last husband (she had three), whom she hated and on whose account she had prayed to God to forget.

Even so, they buried him next to Lorenza, and I wonder, superstitiously, if she recognizes him now, lying in the earth beside her. But wondering this is ridiculous, since I don't believe in such things. Still, I shiver, even in the heat.

When Bibi finds out they've buried him next to her, she sucks in air and whistles. She says, "She wouldn't have liked that. *Hubiera protestado.*"

"This is the first time you've been to see her grave?" I ask.

"That's right."

"But she's been dead for five years!"

Bibi shakes her head and looks at me like I am speaking Martian. "That's what you don't understand, Lisa."

"What?"

"That she's not dead—that she'll never be dead."

She's right. That's what I don't understand.


It's my last night in Panama, and Bibi and I go downstairs to her neighbor Mirna's apartment for a little party. Mirna, a tiny woman with soft skin and graying hair, is a seamstress from Colombia. She sews for Sandra Sandoval, a famous Panamanian performer who sings with her brother Samy.

After two hours, Bibi's boyfriend José shows up and starts dancing. He drags me off the couch and I try not to step on his feet. Bibi orders Mirna's son to get some rum and limes, and the next thing I know everyone is tipsy.

Bibi turns to them, points to me, and says in slurred Spanish, "This one doesn't believe in God."

There is a dramatic silence after they all suck in air, gasping in shock. Great.

"*Es que necesito prueba,*" ("I need proof.") I say.

Before I can qualify this statement any further, which might not even be possible, since I am half gone on *mojitos,* everyone in the room is offering up experiential evidence to support the existence of God and telling stories about supernatural occurrences in their respective Latin American countries.

José describes a Cuban method by which butterflies are used to talk to the dead.

Mirna reports seeing a dead man who comes back to life in Colombia.

Bibi spins the familiar Panamanian *Tulivieja* story.

Yolanda, a lady from the Dominican Republic, describes the lights that come out of the tombs of cemeteries at night, but concedes that this happens everywhere.

And Eva, who hasn't said a word all evening, explains all there is to know about witches. An interesting fact about witches is that they can take the form of pigs, turkeys, horses, snakes, and monkeys, but not cats, dogs, or turtles. Eva advises me that if the witch is a monkey it is best to use salt, which will burn it.

"Yes, yes," Mirna interrupts. "But if you are walking down the street and see a pig on the corner who keeps giving you dirty looks, you may be seeing a witch in disguise."

Eva continues, "And if every day the same pig gives you the same evil look, then you may be sure of it. Once you are sure, you must scoop a handful of grain—be it rice or wheat or corn—and approach the disguised witch and throw the grain at the pig's feet.

"Then you must say: 'I know that you are a witch, and I want you to pick up these grains, one by one.'"

At this point the witch should turn back into a witch, but she will be naked. And due to her need for order, she will be compelled to pick up each grain, one by one, because she will not be able to bear seeing them scattered and disordered in the street.

I am not sure what happens after she finishes picking up the grain, but I imagine by then I would be long gone.

"Where did you learn this?" I ask.

"*El cura.*"

"Your *priest* told you to do this?" I ask.

"*Claro,*" she says, as if to say "Who else?"

"Have you ever had to follow his advice?" I ask.

"No." She shakes her head and sips on her *mojito*, daintily picking a mint leaf from between her teeth. *"Gracias a Dios, no."*

My mother is starting to make sense.


The next morning, Bibi and I have a tearful farewell, promising each other we'll write more often in the future. I hope we do.

*"Que Dios te bendiga,"* she says in parting, and I feel blessed.

As I fly back home to California, hung over and tired, I find myself wondering about the in-between-ness of it all. Christian, witch, priest, and witness, you are first one thing, then another. Then you are neither, and then, finally, you are all. You are backward and forward, frontward and back, trying to make sense of it all.

I think fondly of the gold Buddha on my mantel and hope he's not getting too dusty in my absence. I promise myself to give him a good polish when I return, not because I think I will be reborn, saved, or resurrected by the Buddha's power, but because I need, as we all need, to believe in something outside of myself, something greater, something good. I don't believe in God, but I believe in flesh and blood, skin and bone, and our uncanny ability to be two contradictory things at the same time.

Standing in front of the glossy locks of the Panama Canal, Bibi said, "It's a palindrome." It strikes me that I have visited Panama in 2002, the year of the palindrome, and that although this year will pass, I am in it now, straddling two worlds, a fleshly bridge, a divided yet connected being. Panama connects more than oceans, more than continents, more than cultures, waters, and lives. It also moves between and mixes different poles, peoples, religions, and times.

Staring out the window of the airplane at the clouds and oceans below me, I think that each of us is a palindrome made of muscle, made of blood, that reaches back to the past, even as we throw out grappling hooks toward the future. Lorenza, Margarita, my mother, and I—we all started out inside the bellies of bodies of different times, different places, and are products of the "then" as much as of the "now."

When I see my mother, perhaps I will tell her this. I will say, "I do not understand you; perhaps I never will. But I know that you are part of me as surely as we breathe, as surely as we dream." I will take her hands in mine and examine her small palms.

"I am not a witch," I will say. "And I do not believe what you believe. But I recognize your flesh in my hands, your blood in my veins, and the black witch's mole on the back of your neck, which is also on mine. I am your daughter, and you are your mother's daughter, and one day perhaps I will have a daughter, and I will point her backward, even as she moves forward in time, and she will see that she is her mother's daughter, farther and farther back down the line, until it's harder and harder to see us, to see you, to see me, forward to infinity, all the way back to Eve."

# Blending the Red with the White and the Blue

## Margaret Gelbwasser

I was eleven when I first encountered the Russian/Jewish/American dilemma. We were doing a social studies project, and our teacher wanted us to draw the flag that symbolized our heritage. For me, that was a gold hammer and sickle on a blood red background. The red overpowered the whole image.

That night, I told my father about the assignment. I wasn't surprised when he made a face of utter disgust, since he and my mother had lived the stories that I had only heard. In these stories, my paternal grandfather was taken to prison, in the middle of the night, for receiving talliths, Jewish prayer shawls, in the mail. Another story was of my maternal grandfather, at age six, bearing witness to the hanging of his father, simply because he was Jewish. The stories continued—of lit Sabbath candles, hushed voices praying, shades pulled closed, starvation, more hangings. I was not to draw the flag that represented everything we'd fled, everything my family hated. My father wanted me to draw the Israeli flag because, according to him, that was the home of our people. My teacher, who wanted the assignment to be simple and to fit within her notion of a melting pot and neatly outlined bulletin board, said that I was not Israeli. In the end, we compromised and I drew a flag of the United Nations. Two other Russian Jewish students in my class did the same.

My family and I fled the former Soviet Union in 1979 with fifty thousand other Russian Jewish refugees. I was three when we arrived in the United States. My only memories of Belarus are stories I have heard. Growing up, I was always reminded that being a Jew was our only identity in Russia. People would look at our dark hair and facial features and think *Jew*. Even our passports said "Jew." My father often rubbed his knuckles and described the fistfights he'd gotten into for being called "Jew boy." So I understood the Jewish identity as something one should defend, coming away with permanent scars if necessary. I understood that America was supposed to be the land that provided all the freedoms we did not have in the former Soviet Union. Therefore, being an American was important, too. And being Russian? This was also a part of me; I knew this because, at home, my parents, grandparents, and I all spoke Russian. On holidays, when elaborate meals were prepared, we ate typical Russian fare, such as herring under a blanket, salad *olivyeh* (a meat and vegetable mix), borscht, and stuffed chicken skins, alongside the turkey and cranberry sauce and yams. But since we didn't speak Russian outside the house, I didn't think that this part of my background warranted the same pride as my Jewish and American identities. These thoughts were confirmed when people asked my parents if they were Russian. "No, we're Jewish," they'd answer, or, "No, we're Americans." So, while I couldn't completely comprehend this separation, I did see that the Russian side of me was not something anyone fought over or strived to protect. I concluded that it couldn't be that important.

As I got older, I began to understand the division my parents faced. When I entered junior high in 1988, a group of boys took to calling me a "commie." Some of these boys were in my Hebrew school class, and it baffled me that they thought I was any less Jewish than they were. Others lived near my house and saw my family hang our American flag on patriotic holidays; sometimes, our flag was out when theirs wasn't. Yet, they thought I was less of an American, too. It didn't happen every day, and seemed to be provoked by the study of the Cold War, but I went home in tears each time. After misinterpreting a lesson on McCarthyism, two male classmates ran around my lunch table shouting, "Reds! Reds! Down with the Reds!" My friend Elena stared at her sandwich, but I thought they just didn't understand and attempted to explain the truth. I tried telling them that communism was something we escaped, the source of so many evils done to my family and others. They were silent for a few seconds, probably shocked that I had even said something. Then, they took up their chant again, to a different table of Russian students. A week later, another group of boys came to school with *Rocky* t-shirts on. When they passed me, they pointed to Stallone's face and said, "Take that, Russki." Thinking they were the lunchroom kids who didn't get it, I started explaining that I wasn't a commie and that Russian Jews living in the United States didn't want to have anything to do with the government they'd left behind. But they walked away singing the *Rocky* theme loudly. I knew then that they did not want to understand; they wanted to laugh, to assert their "patriotism." They wanted to be like Rocky or Rambo and beat down the bad Russians. After a while, I gave up explaining and also stopped wearing anything red.

In high school, one of my friends insisted that we speak Russian when she didn't want others to understand what we were saying. I refused. When people asked me where I was from, I always answered "Brooklyn," which was where I lived before my family moved to New Jersey. "Where are you from *originally?*" they'd press. I would feign confusion and change the subject. If a teacher learned that I was Russian and attempted to use the few Russian words she knew, I'd claim to have forgotten the language, "since I immigrated at such a young age." One Hebrew school teacher insisted on asking me my impressions of Russian landmarks like the Kremlin or the Hermitage, sites I didn't remember. Every week, he'd question me about a new place, or the cost of Russian goods, or the lack of decent toilet paper, or whether I'd enjoyed the schools there. Although I repeatedly explained that leaving a country at age three did not give me access to such knowledge, he was not daunted. I quickly learned that "misunderstanding" questions about my background was the easier route.

In college, things changed, and I learned to value my Russian heritage. College brought with it diversity and students who were more tolerant of other cultures, a quality my small, suburban hometown lacked. Though I had read some Russian authors in high school, reading the works of Dostoyevsky, Lermontov, and Pushkin in my college literature classes gave me a new perspective on Russian history and culture. In college, teachers and students enthusiastically discussed Russian landmarks and did not expect me to have a greater-than-average knowledge of the subject. And, rather than mocking my heritage, my peers longed to hear about growing up Russian in America and even stayed after class to tell me new Russian words they'd learned. In turn, I became interested in my experiences as well and felt proud that I was different from others.

Recent *Sopranos* episodes featuring the Russian mob and Tony's one-legged Russian girlfriend remind me that the stereotypes are still out there; only now, they seem fewer or less hurtful than before. Sometimes, if people appear receptive, I tell them of my family's Russian experiences and the kinds of memories young refugees like me have. And, I often wear my favorite sweater. It is soft, a V-neck, and it's red.

# Caught between Worlds: A Pakistani-Muslim Adolescence in America

### Maliha Masood

"Maliha! Come and say your *maghrib* prayers. The sun is going down fast and you're late as usual," my mother's voice trailed from the balcony of our sixth-story apartment near the Arabian Sea. But I was barely listening, too busy playing hide-and-seek with my buddies Asma and Faiza to bother about praying. When the sky was drained of all its color, I sauntered back home armed with a pack of flimsy lies to justify my negligence.

My favorite lie was that my watch had stopped ticking and I couldn't tell the time. But that didn't explain why I had also ignored the *Azaan*, the call to prayer, blaring from the neighborhood mosque in a scratchy baritone. The only true explanation was that I was too young to absorb the tenets of my religion, among which the five daily prayers ranks the highest. Though Pakistan is an Islamic country, I had attended a secular Zoroastrian private school. My parents did not impose Islam through rigorous training. But they instilled in me the importance of faith. It harnessed a portable inner axis of self-awareness that I brought with me to the land of milk and honey.

In June 1982, I boarded a plane at Karachi International Airport on a one-way ticket. Two days later, I would arrive in Seattle, Washington, along with my father, mother, and two younger siblings. Why Seattle? Blame it on the evergreens and Mount Rainier. My dad had fallen in love with glossy pictures of them on a calendar of the great Pacific Northwest. He talked about fresh clean air and tidy sidewalks. He envisioned cool raindrops instead of tropical heat waves. He craved nonstop hot running water, electric stoves, and a postal system not partial to confiscating international mail. He actually wanted to pay taxes.

My father was tired of broken things in a broken country. So he decided to transport his family to America to start a brand-new life. At the time, I did not fully understand the ramifications of his decision. All I knew was that we were leaving Pakistan, the country where I was born and raised until the age of eleven. Flying twelve thousand miles from east to west, I felt that I was in a galactic time machine.

The first few months, we stayed with my dad's sister. She lived in a house made entirely of wood, called a rambler. It made me think of an extra-long matchbox. There were raccoons in the front yard where a boy tossed a newspaper every morning. He would snicker at my outfit—baggy, knee-length shirt and billowy trousers fitted at the ankles: the traditional *shalwar kameez* that I had worn back in Karachi. People gave me strange looks when I wore this outfit in Seattle. I begged my mother to buy me some American clothes so I could appear halfway normal. She took me to Kmart, where I picked out a checkered cowboy shirt and dark blue jeans with roller skates stenciled on the back pocket. When the cashier couldn't understand my mom's broken English, she looked at me to translate. After she finished ringing us up, I asked her if she could direct us to the nearest "petrol pump." The cashier popped her wad of pink bubblegum and rolled her eyes. She thought I was trying to pull her leg. But the foreigner in me had no idea that I should have asked for a "gas station." I was in linguistic limbo.

Growing up in Karachi, I had to juggle three languages. I spoke my native tongue, Urdu, with my mother and the servants, and flaunted the Queen's English with my dad. He had been raised and educated in India, just like my mother. After they married, they settled in Pakistan. There, I was subject to weekly visits by an elderly *maulvi*, or religious scholar, who came by our colonial-style bungalow to teach me how to read and write Arabic. I recited all thirty chapters of the Holy Koran three different times before I hit puberty, I didn't understand the guttural syllables that I parroted after *maulvi saab* every Friday afternoon. Even though I didn't learn the language, it was important that I had read the Koran from start to finish in its original Arabic version. It assured more *barkaat*—reward in the hereafter—according to my aunties in Bombay.


"You mean you can't speak any Arabic? But aren't you a Muslim?"

My very first friend in America was a Jewish girl named Rachel Cohen. We sat next to each other in Mrs. Wright's sixth-grade class and compared our latest shades of fingernail polish. She preferred bold reds, while I leaned toward pastels. Rachel had never known a Muslim before, but she harbored expectations about what a Muslim was supposed to look and act like. For one thing, I should have known Arabic. For another, I should have had my head covered. But these things were not stressed in Karachi during my childhood. I smiled at Rachel and told her that Muslims come in all shapes and sizes, in a range of colors and textures. Just like nail polish.

My life in America was getting started, and I quickly began to speak English with a flagrant American accent, but from the very beginning, I felt off-centered. My fair complexion meant people took me for Caucasian. This caused resentment among my South Asian classmates who couldn't blend in as easily as I did on account of their darker skin tones. To compensate for this betrayal, I would recite the Pledge of Allegiance with a more heated fervor every morning in class. *And to the republic for which it stands: one nation, under God, indivisible, with liberty and justice for all.*

I was old enough to know that not everyone got a piece of liberty and justice in the great U.S. of A. But I did not internalize issues of "race," "ethnicity," or "minority"—even when I had to fill out forms and darken the bubble with a No. 2 pencil next to the word "Pacific Islander/Asian" for racial identification, the closest option available. There was no bubble for a Pakistani Muslim American girl who looked Italian. But I didn't feel so different in my day-to-day existence. I woke up, ate cereal, went to school, came home for dinner, and worked on my homework sprawled in front of the television before going to bed and repeating the cycle the next day and the next. On weekends, our family would pack sandwiches and a thermos of milky chai and head to the nearest county park. We basked in the fresh air and tepid sunshine that doused memories of the prickly monsoon heat of Karachi. We acclimatized to America. We harmonized with our adopted homeland. We ignored the hyphenated identities towing an invisible undercurrent in our lives.

By the time I got to middle school, in the mid-1980s, the American in me was in full swing. The sliding doors of my bedroom closet at home were littered with posters of Duran Duran. I knew all the lyrics to the song "Union of the Snake." Sometimes, my grandmother, who also lived with us, would pound on the adjoining wall as a signal for me to turn down the volume on my boom box. Her taste in music did not extend to Simon and company. But Granny loved watching reruns of *M\*A\*S\*H*, and would even join me for my favorite sitcom—*The Facts of Life*. I was learning my own "facts" as a seventh grader. A boy named Jeff became the object of a secret crush. He was too shy to look in my direction in our homeroom class—much less to be aware of my existence. I also got an after-school job at a department store when I was fourteen. It made my parents happy, since they didn't want me to live on handouts. Hard work and earning an honest wage were the American values they wanted me to adopt. But at the same time, they would never let me bask in full-blown independence by going to my friends' slumber parties or looking into out-of-state colleges. It was considered too *modern* a move for a traditional Muslim family. I was expected to live at home with my parents until I got married. Living in America was not going to diminish the cultural baggage we had imported from Pakistan. If I thought I was like everybody else around me, I was fooling myself.

"I will write a note to your teacher. Then you will be excused from taking part in this silly exercise." My father reached for his silver Cross pen.

"But I don't want to be excused! I want to learn how to swim! Why can't I learn how to swim?"

"You know very well that it is not right to wear a bathing suit and show your body in front of strangers," my father insisted.

"Strangers! They are my friends. I know all their names. They are hardly strangers!"

"Aren't some of those friends boys?" he asked without lifting his eyes from the note he was now completely engaged in writing.

"Well, yes. It is a coed school, in case you hadn't noticed." I rolled my eyes.

"Don't get smart with me. You are not allowed to swim in front of members of the opposite sex. It is against our religion. Plain and simple."

"Where does it say that in the Koran? Show me *right now* the actual words that forbid me to swim!" I was nearly out of breath.

I removed the holy book from the top shelf of the bookcase. It was wrapped in a soft cotton cloth with a cross-stitched border of little birds. My father took the Koran from my hands and restored it to its place.

"Stop being so silly. You are an intelligent girl and you know the rules. It's no use arguing about it."

"Who's making the rules, you or God?" I shot back.

"Maliha!"

It was not a good sign when a normally benign-looking face grew red with fury. I tried a new strain of logic.

"What about the gymkhana in Karachi? I used to play tennis there in short skirts with *boys!* How come it didn't matter what I wore?"

"That was entirely different. We were in our own country among our own people. Now you are in America. You must learn to respect your culture. It is important to remember where you are coming from. If not, you will be lost. You will start getting into all sorts of trouble like these American kids. You will bring shame upon our family. Is that why we brought you here? To bring us shame, to cause your mother and I to worry all the time that you will get into the wrong crowds and adopt their bad habits . . ." My dad's voice trailed off.

"I only want to learn how to swim." My tears blurred the cornflower pattern on the tiles of our kitchen floor.


A week later, I handed an ivory-colored envelope to Mrs. Lungstrom, my ninth-grade gym teacher. She nodded and smiled graciously. Her cultural sensitivity dissuaded her from questioning my father's wishes, though she probably did not understand why "Islamic modesty" got in the way of swimming lessons. She probably chalked it up to a Muslim peculiarity, something to condone and accept in Seattle's progressive culture. But to me, there was nothing "Muslim" about my father's note. Religion was the pretext for covering up fears and insecurities of cultural assimilation, a dilemma common to immigrants from all strands of faith and belief systems. I sat on the bleachers and watched my friends frolic in the pool.

By my senior year in high school, I had given up reasoning with my father when it came to Muslim dos and don'ts. His leniency did not extend toward matters of dress. Not only was I forbidden to wear a bathing suit, I was also not allowed to wear sleeveless shirts, tight t-shirts, jeans, shorts, or skirts. Anything that exposed the length of my arms or legs or revealed my open back or midriff was strictly off-limits. As a gawky teenager, I was comfortable in baggy clothes, so the dress code did not create a major inconvenience. But during a heat wave, I longed to wear a tank top and plaid cotton shorts like the other kids at school. It was embarrassing to be the only person in the entire school covering her legs with full-length pants. When my classmates asked me if I was hot, I tried to picture snowstorms and pretended to shiver. I got used to them snickering behind my back, poking fun at my strange ways.

Then one day I received an epiphany in the girls' bathroom. I was standing in line with my legs crossed to control the urge to pee when I heard the rustling of a plastic bag in one of the occupied stalls. Then I heard an elastic band snap and a loud "ouch!" I bent my head and peeked underneath the door. A pair of slim brown legs clouded my vision. I stared harder. The feet belonging to those legs slipped into white strappy sandals with kitten heels. Elastic snapped. The girl inside the stall giggled. Then the door clicked open. My mouth opened wide. In front of me stood a petite, olive-complexioned girl in a yellow gingham-print halter top with an elasticized bodice paired with snow white shorts hiked up to mid-thigh. Her bare legs were smooth as cinnamon sticks. The thing that really shocked me was the gold locket with stylized Arabic lettering dangling from her neck.

"N-u-r-e-e-n." I spelled out her name.

"That's right." She flashed a quick smile.

"You're new, aren't you?"

"Yeah, we just moved here from Tempe, Arizona. I just started classes a week ago."

"Uh-huh." I was enraptured with the sight of Nureen staining her lips with pink gloss.

"So where are you from originally?" I asked.

"India. Can't you tell from my face?"

"So we're first cousins."

"United in sisterhood!"

"*Muslim* sisterhood!" I added.

Nureen nodded and flashed another smile. She started to dab some blue shadow on her lids. My head spun.

"Uhh, if you're Muslim, then why are you dressed like that?"

"My parents would kill me if they saw me like this. But I only wear these clothes at school or when I go out with my friends. My parents don't know. It's a secret."

It was news to me that I could live a double life.

"But don't you feel weird, sneaking around like that and betraying your parents?"

Nureen laughed. "Who said anything about betrayal? I'm not trying to hurt them. Look, girl. Wearing shorts is not a crime in my book. We're in America now." She stretched her halter top taut against her skin.

Nureen and I became fast friends. With her encouragement, I started coming to school an hour early to allow enough time for my daily makeover. We would meet in the girls' bathroom and twitter with excitement as we changed into our disguises. Nureen zipped up the mint green sundress I exchanged for a pair of baggy navy chinos and my brother's extra-large long-sleeved cement-colored crewneck t-shirt. When I twirled around for the inspection, my glamorous new friend jumped up and down and clapped her hands. She showed me how to wear frosted eye shadow and line my eyes with black kohl. She lent me her *Seventeen* magazines and cutouts of lingerie ads. We shared a locker where we stashed two small duffle bags containing our smuggled treasures. Our friends started to notice. Boys called me a babe. We were invited to weekend parties and off-campus lunches at Dairy Queen. The coolness factor was not just the domain of cheerleaders. It extended to Nureen and myself as we learned to navigate the slippery slope between our cultural dualities without falling through the cracks.

On those rare occasions when I consider myself an average stateside citizen, it is hard to accept the fact that I never learned to swim simply because I was a Muslim girl attending an American public school. If I had really been determined to hold my breath under water and master the breaststroke, I could have found alternative ways, such as an all-girls swim session at our neighborhood aquatic center or even a private club for Muslim sisters at some rich lady's house. But I did not want "special treatment," as if I were handicapped. So I obeyed my parents' wishes to respect and honor our Islamic heritage in Seattle, where we had been living for seven years.

Now I realize that my parents were simply preserving cultural norms that had nothing to do with religion itself, but were still justified on religious grounds. The blurring of culture and religion is endemic not only to Islam. But when Islam is transported to America, it becomes vulnerable to outside influences that are feared to dilute its "identity." So Muslim immigrants become extra-cautious and seek security by building fences. They prevent their daughters from wearing bathing suits and shorts. They cloak their faith in dogma until dogma is all that remains of faith. This paints a portrait of an intolerant, backward Islam to non-Muslims, who often react to what they see with fear and suspicion.

But none of this is *my* Islam. What I love most about my religion is the freedom it allows me to use my own mind. The Koran repeatedly mentions the importance of human reasoning, or *aql*. It burdens me with the responsibility to make choices in line with my own intellect.

In other words, there is no intermediary between God and me. In my view, there is a big difference between the politics of Islam and the spirit of Islam. The politicized version is a galaxy removed from the living, breathing spirituality that pulses through my veins. This spiritual side has taught me to value what is on the inside rather than focus on surface appearances for validity.

Now that I'm older, it no longer bothers me *not* to wear figure-revealing clothing or swim in front of men, even though I could do those things if I wanted. My parents would probably still mind. But they wouldn't chastise me for exercising my own judgment. Not if they believe in the empowering and liberating Islam that I will entrust to my American-born kids.

# (UN)AMERICAN

## Patricia Justine Tumang

"YOU SIMPLY CANNOT BE AMERICAN," the man standing on the street in Mombasa told me as I walked out of a restaurant one scorching day. It was several weeks into my study-abroad program on Swahili culture and history, in the fall of 2000. I was the only Filipino American student out of a group of twelve, most of whom were white, middle-class Americans.

The sun shone brightly above me as I strained to see the man's face. His eyes revealed sincerity and curiosity. People in the area had grown accustomed to seeing our group of American students walking around town. Since we were staying near Fort Jesus, just around the corner from the restaurant, those who spoke English often approached us to ask questions. Today was no different, but I was alone and wasn't in a leisurely mood. My stomach was full from the chicken *biriani* I had quickly eaten in my rush to make it to class on time. My breath, reeking of garlic, cumin, and onions, felt stilted. Although I had grown accustomed to being an object of profound curiosity to many Kenyans since my arrival, the question "Where are you from?" continued to make me feel defensive.

"I was born in America," I retorted, wanting that to be enough of an answer. It never was, but it would be a more complicated matter to explain that "American" meant more than blond hair and blue eyes. Besides, I was already running late for class.

Eyeing me carefully, the man said, "You speak like an American, but you don't look like one."

Sweat began to trickle down my face as if a light rain were falling. The day was as hot as ever, and the heat felt foreign and overbearing.

"I'm Asian," I said, trying out a different answer. *Perhaps he wanted to know my ethnicity.*

The man looked at me quizzically and a smile began to emerge, his upper lip receding like a curtain to reveal a line of perfectly straight white teeth.

"You don't look Asian or American." Pointing to a man on the other side of the street, he said, "Look at that man, he is Asian."

The man across the street was tall and broad-shouldered. He wore a simple gray *kofia* made of plain cotton on his head. His long khaki robe draped his entire body. *He must be hot,* I thought. As he crossed the street toward us, I quickly glanced at his features. His brown complexion was ruddy and flushed, and his black eyebrows were bushy and thick. His nose, long and angled, was bulbous at the tip. His eyelashes were long and wispy like a spider's legs.

"He is an Asian of Indian descent," I replied, feeling impatient with the conversation.

"He is Asian and you're not," the man said confidently.

"Yes, he is Asian, and I am Asian, too," I said, "and I am also American."

The man laughed at me, his dark brown eyes glittering in the oppressive sun. "Perhaps you did live in America since your English is so good."

*I was born in America and English is my first language.*

Heat rose to my cheeks like spreading fever. I grew up in Los Angeles, a city with a huge immigrant population. Although there are many first- and second-generation families in Los Angeles, ignorance and prejudice are omnipresent. On the streets of L.A., whenever I was asked, "Where are you from?" it was usually a signifier of racism by white people who assumed that I was a foreigner—other, and un-American. And my American accent was often the impetus for insults disguised as compliments: "You speak English so well—like an American."

Halfway around the world, I was in a similar bind. Being patient with the Kenyan man reminded me of my passivity with white people in the United States. As a young Asian female, I was taught by my family to be polite. The question "Where are you from?" seemed innocent enough. However, like a mosquito bite that begins to itch well after one is bitten, I didn't realize until later that the question was meant to identify me as an outsider, someone who never was and could never be American.

"I must go because I'm late for class," I said to the man, regaining my composure. *Did he see me flinch when he insisted that I was neither Asian nor American?*

"*Asante sana mwanafunzi,*" ("Thank you student.") the man said to me as I ran hastily down the gravel road toward Fort Jesus.

In the coastal region of Kenya, where Kiswahili is the predominant spoken language, white people are called "*Mzungu,*" which literally means "foreigner." It is a derogatory term that could be applied to anyone non-Kenyan, but it is mostly said to white people. The word "*Mchina,*" meaning person of Chinese descent, is what people usually called me. "*Mchina,*" they said, pointing to me.

*"Unatoka wapi?"* ("Where are you from?") one young Kenyan boy with a caramel complexion asked me. I had just arrived at the Pate district in Faza Island after a grueling, four-hour boat ride on a massive dhow from Lamu Town, one hour away by plane from Mombasa. According to my host mother Miriamu, foreigners do not often visit Pate. As soon as I disembarked, young children clung to my waist like rustling fabric from a swishing ball gown. The children moved with me as I struggled to keep up with Miriamu, who was ten paces ahead.

*"Unatoka wapi?"* the boy repeated his question.

The other children looked to me for an answer. The boy who asked was a brave one. While the other kids were just as curious, they were also shy. A young Kenyan girl in a pink dress smiled at me and looked away when I made eye contact. All of them were simply content to stare at me, eyeing me as if I were a riddle that they wanted to figure out.

*"Ninatoka* America," I said. *"Nina jua* Patty." After two months of intensive language training in Kiswahili, I felt confident in written exams, but the thought of speaking aloud intimidated me. *They're just kids*, I thought to myself, *act natural.*

Another little girl stepped in and declared, *"Unatoka China!"* The other children sang out in a belted chorus, *"Mchina! Wewe ni Mchina!"*

*"Mimi si Mchina,"* I said uneasily, knowing that the situation was hopeless.

The boy who asked me the question introduced me to his little brother. "He is three and I am five," the boy said. Turning to the little brother, I smiled and extended my hand. The boy was unduly shy and, instead of shaking my hand, opted to hide behind his brother.

"He has a present for you," the older brother said. He pushed his younger brother closer to me. Standing in front of me, the young boy was striking. He had a light complexion, and sandy brown curls graced his small head. In the United States, the boy could easily be mistaken for being half black and half white. In Kenya, racial and ethnic mixing was common, especially along the coast where, in the sixteenth and seventeenth centuries, trade, immigration, and colonization had brought Indians, Arabs, Portuguese, Ethiopian refugees, and the British to the port cities. This multiracial mixing contributed to variations in skin tone, eye color, and hair texture, which reminded me of the colonial history of the Philippines.

My ancestors are descendants of the Negritos of Malaysia, the Spaniards, the Chinese, and the Americans. My assumption that all Africans looked the same—dark brown skin, emaciated torsos, and narrow faces—was dispelled on the day of my arrival when I met Kenyans of a diverse range of complexions and statures. Kenyans didn't look anything like the Africans in the Sally Struthers infomercials of my adolescence that came on late at night and featured starving children from third-world countries. Nor did they look like the African people shown in *National Geographic* magazines, where, if Kenyans were featured, it was the Masai tribe, whose dark skin contrasted with their colorful beaded jewelry. The few media images of Africans in America perpetuated the stereotype that all African people looked the same. Although I was attending college in New York City, where people of all races and cultures mixed, these powerful stereotypes pervaded my psyche. If I had previously assumed that all Kenyans looked the same, why should it surprise me that they would think that all Asians looked the same?

"Give her the present," the older brother insisted. The young boy smiled at me and giggled. Other children started to giggle along with him.

He approached me and opened his closed fist. On his palm rested a crumpled-up piece of paper that looked like a bubblegum wrapper.

"*Asante sana*," I thanked the boy. He looked at me beaming, proud of his gift.

"*Yeye ni Mchina*," ("She is Chinese.") another girl whispered to a group of children who had just joined the scene.

"Open it," the older brother commanded.

I carefully took the paper, a small one-by-two-inch Bazooka Joe bubblegum wrapper, and unfolded it neatly between my fingers. I looked at the wrapper on my palm with familiarity. After reading the cartoon, I said again to the younger brother, "*Asante sana.*"

The older brother stepped in and said, "But you must turn it over to see the picture of your brother."

"No, no, *sina kaka*," ("I don't have a brother.") I insisted.

The younger brother took the wrapper from my hand and turned it over. On the back side was a colored picture of Bruce Lee with his fists in the air and his leg fully extended in a karate kick.

A look of shock must have registered on my face, because all of the children started laughing. The young boy smiled, looking very proud of himself.

"*Ana jua* Bruce Lee," I told them his name. "*Yeye ni Mchina.*" ("He is Chinese, but I am not.")

"*Ninatoka* America," I repeated. The children looked at me, confused.

"America?" one child asked, unsure of what I was telling him.

"*Mchina*," another child interrupted, pointing her finger at me.

Only five minutes had gone by, but I felt tired of explaining myself. The children called after me, saying, "*Mchina!*" when I walked away to rejoin Miriamu, who was sitting on her sister's porch several feet away.

Miriamu listened while I expressed my frustration. "They just haven't seen someone different in a long time, and they are trying to make friends with you," she reassured me. "Not a lot of tourists come this way. The children are not used to seeing someone who isn't from Pate."

Miriamu's explanation calmed me at the time, but afterward I began to think more critically about the young boy showing me the picture of Bruce Lee. *What does this image mean to him? To me? Why did he feel that it was important to show the picture to me?*

During the course of my travels in Kenya, I continued to be an instant celebrity. Something in my eyes gave me away. The guessing game oscillated between Chinese and Japanese. Along the Lamu seafront, where many Kenyan seafarers and tour guides baited customers for morning sailing trips to the outer islands, I was regaled with "*Arigato!*"

and "*Sayonara!*" On some occasions I stopped to say, "I don't speak Japanese, I'm an American," but my words fell on deaf ears. Although I recognized many of the seafarers, as I'm sure they recognized me, they continued to speak to me in rudimentary Japanese.

The fact that no one believed that I was an American was not unusual or far-fetched. Many Kenyans believe that all Americans are white. The limited American media that reaches the coastal region features TV shows that are reflective of American popular culture—shows that legitimize and promote the image of Americans as a homogenous racial group.

However, there was one contemporary Asian actor that many Kenyans knew and identified with.

Since very few people owned TVs in Lamu, my friends and I watched American movies in the only public movie theater in the town. It was down a dirt road on the outskirts of the town center. The theater was very different from American movie theaters. It was a modest dark room in a wooden shack with a small TV in the back. There were forty metal folding chairs that were falling apart at the hinges lined in neat rows. People's laughter and conversation gradually permeated the room like a soft echo that gathers volume in a cave. Cigarette smoke billowed like a hazy fog and shielded the screen. The smoke, however, could not hide the unmistakable image of Jackie Chan doing karate kicks. The darkness would swallow me up as my eyes locked on the screen. I was thankful for the blanket of darkness that kept me invisible. There were no other women, Asians, or Americans in the theater.

*Rush Hour*, a town favorite, featured Jackie Chan as Inspector Lee, a stubborn detective whose skill in martial arts earns him respect but brings him trouble. The image of Jackie Chan doing karate kicks stayed with me as my Kenyan friends improvised martial arts moves after the movie ended. We were walking back to the seafront when my friend Kazungu said, "I want to be just like Jackie Chan."

Recalling the picture of Bruce Lee that the young boy in Pate had shared with me, I began to think of the stereotypes of Asians that were being perpetuated through American media. The only popular images of Asians in the media that reached Kenya were male kung fu stars. Bruce Lee, known to the world for his cunning martial arts skills in his famous movie *Enter the Dragon*, is a popular symbol of Asian American masculinity. Touted for his prowess at kung fu, Bruce Lee, much like Jackie Chan, has come to represent a common stereotype in the Asian American community—that Asian men are asexual, machinelike, and absolutely un-American.

Trying to combine my two cultures was like mixing oil with water—no matter how much I tried to mix my Filipino and American identities, they always separated.

This is what I struggled with as Kenyans questioned my self-identification as Asian American. The irony was that I harbored more doubts about my identity than any of them could guess. When I was a child I wanted more than anything to be accepted both by my family and by my American peers at school.

Bringing packed lunches to elementary school signaled my difference. Although many of my classmates were kids of color—black, Latino, and Asian—white students viewed anything not considered American as strange. Instead of baloney and cheese sandwiches, a typical American lunch, I ate rice and my mother's chicken adobo. "You eat rice with every meal?" a white classmate once asked me. "Yes," I responded. *Didn't everybody?* "That's weird," she said. It wasn't weird to me. "What is that stuff?" she asked. "It's adobo," I said. A confused look on her face told me that she didn't understand. "It's chicken," I added, "and it's really good." Feeling satisfied with my answer, my classmate continued eating her lunch. I hadn't realized until that point that no one knew what chicken adobo was. Suddenly I felt like an outsider.

And in some ways, I felt like an outsider at home, too. Growing up, I felt different from my Filipino parents, who immigrated to the United States a year before I was born. I didn't grow up speaking Tagalog like my parents did. When I was a little girl, my parents exchanged audio-tapes with our relatives in the Philippines instead of calling or writing letters. When our relatives sent us audiotapes, their voices filled our ste-reo with sounds that were unfamiliar to me. Uncles and aunts spoke in different dialects. When they addressed my mom, high-pitched voices filled the speakers. I could almost see their mouths curl to form a cir-cle with their lips, repeating the vowel *o*. My mother laughed when she heard their voices. They spoke Tagalog to my father because he didn't understand my mother's native dialect of Ilonggo. Tagalog is rhythmic and sharp, like the sound of water collapsing against a heavy rock.

English was inserted only sporadically, so I was left in the dark. "What are they saying?" I'd ask my mom, persistently tugging on her sleeve. "Shhhh," she'd say and hug me affectionately. "Please quiet, I want to hear what they're saying. It's just *tsismis* anyway." A smile spread over her face as she listened to the latest gossip. Sometimes tears streamed down her cheeks when she heard her mother speak. What happy news was shared? Did something bad happen to our family? I didn't know how to articulate such questions yet.

The joys and longings my parents experienced were transferred to me as I sang unabashedly in Tagalog. In fact, the only Tagalog I knew was from Filipino songs on tapes sent by my mother's brothers, who were musicians. The Filipino ballads that we listened to in the house became part of the background as my mother cooked Filipino food and I did homework at night. My mother told me that the songs were about longing and heartache. I'd sing the tunes as easily as I would "Old Mc-Donald Had a Farm," and my parents would tape me and send these audiotapes to our relatives in the Philippines. I belted out the chorus to the Filipino songs with gusto and feeling, wondering if my voice could carry through to the other side, seven thousand miles across ocean and land, to the place that my parents called home.

I can only imagine how my relatives would have reacted to me sing-ing. Tita Carina, my mother's sister-in-law, would have said, "Look at how cute she is, she actually knows all of the words." Tito Eddieboy, one of my mother's brothers, would have laughed and felt proud since the songs I sang were his favorites by the Filipino singer Basil Valdez. I wonder if, while listening to the tapes, they noticed my American accent. I wonder if it occurred to them that I had no idea what the lyrics meant.

Our audiotapes became extended dialogues that replaced expensive phone calls. My uncles would make *tugon*, which in Ilonggo means to make a request, and it was usually for name-brand shirts, such as Lacoste or Polo; Hormel corned-beef hash; Spam; Whitman's chocolates; and American music.

Tita Carina's voice was singsong and childlike as she tried imitating me. "Oh my god, Patricia. I am so American now. Dude." My parents laughed, even though I didn't think it was funny. A large part of me felt ashamed that I couldn't relate to my relatives in the same way that my parents did. I wanted to feel a connection to my family and to Filipino culture.

I was Filipino in a different way from my family. I didn't know how to speak Tagalog; I didn't understand any of their stories and jokes. The America I grew up in was made of Barbie dolls, McDonald's, and Saturday-morning cartoons like *Thundercats*, *Smurfs*, and *Lady Lovely Locks*. But I didn't feel that this America resonated wholly with who I was. Certainly none of these cartoon characters represented my bilingual family. The two identities that I was struggling to unite—American and Filipino—were separate and distinct.

My family in the Philippines thought that I spoke too fast. My grandmother complained to my mother that "Patricia's English is so American. She talks like she's chewing her words!" At school I was the girl with the weird lunches. Later, as an adult, coming out as queer further marginalized me. I didn't intend to marry a man and conceive children in the traditional way that my parents approved of. They saw my coming out as an indication that they had failed as parents. "Maybe it's these American values that you acquired," my mother said. "You think you can do anything."

The America that I grew up in was not a safe and secure place for a

child of immigrant parents. Although my parents did assimilate well—
they learned to speak American English without a hint of an accent
and made enough money to live very comfortably—I did not escape the
trauma of racism, prejudice, and homophobia.

As a child I remember a common rhyme that my younger cousins and I would sing to one another. We learned it at school, and it
went something like, "Chinese, Japanese, Indian chief." When we said
"Chinese," my cousins and I lifted the outer edges of our eyelids so that
they slanted upward. When we said "Japanese," we pushed the edges
downward. We folded our arms across our chests when we said "Indian
chief." At the age of seven I identified with this rhyme without realizing
its racist implications. My Filipino eyes, which were big and round, also
slanted toward the edges and were in between what I pictured Chinese
and Japanese eyes to look like. Identifying with this rhyme reflected
how I felt as an outsider.

In Kenya, many people assumed that I was heterosexual. I came
out to close friends as queer, but many did not want to believe me.
Some considered queerness an American construction. It was taboo to
talk about issues of sexuality in the Muslim region where I was staying.
People did not want to talk about women being together sexually. Passing for heterosexual felt really debilitating and contributed to my feeling of invisibility about not being seen as an American.

My experience in Kenya evoked many conflicting feelings. I wanted
to be visible. Feeling like an outsider echoed my experience growing up
in the United States. Being marginalized as a queer woman of color
from an immigrant Filipino family contributes to feelings of powerlessness and rage. However, I am an American with middle-class privileges.
When I travel to third-world countries like Kenya and the Philippines,
my money gives me access to resources and institutions of power. I
struggle with the irony of being on both sides of the coin as I navigate
different geographical, political, and personal terrains.

I also struggle with trying to establish a sense of home. I know that
home is the garlicky smell of my mother's home-cooked chicken adobo;

it is hearing the familiar hybrid of Tagalog mixed with English. It is feeling safe in my girlfriend's arms. It means accepting myself for all that I am, including the contradictions and struggles that make me human. I struggle with a divided culture and identity. This divide taught me that speaking English was the only road to success, but the Filipino household that I grew up in reminded me that home was more than the country I was born in. Home is flying across the Pacific Ocean to see my relatives in the Philippines for holiday reunions. It means eating a lot of crispy *pata* and *lechon*, two of my favorite pork dishes, with my family in my *lola's* dining room in the old house on Taft Avenue in Manila. Although my dear grandmother passed away a couple of years ago and the old house was sold, these fond memories stay with me when I think of home. Home is more than where I was born; it is something I carry with me wherever I go.

Since I don't see myself as absolutely American or absolutely Filipino, the obsession with wanting to categorize identity into neat, impermeable definitions is something that doesn't speak to how I view myself. Moving along the gradient between American and Filipino and the hyphenated Filipino-American, my identity is never static. Sometimes, it is a combination of both; at other times one feels more prevalent than the other. Most of the time, I cannot find a single, complete answer. Identities carry a history and legacy that have more meaning than what I tell others I am. Embracing "American" as an identity and rejecting it at the same time, I acknowledge that although I was born in the United States, being American doesn't define all of who I am.

# My Father's Mother Tongue

### Angela Jane Fountas

**The Beginning**

A BLACK-AND-WHITE PHOTOGRAPH of my father and mother sitting at a table covered in a white cloth, a bowl of fruit in the foreground. My father in a crisp white shirt, thin tie, his right hand resting on the table. His left arm around my mother, who leans into him, looking straight into the camera through cat's-eye glasses, the fingers of her right hand intertwined with his.

The fruit bowl and heavy curtains in the background are telling.

The photo was taken at my paternal grandparents' home, before they returned to Greece, in the early years of my parents' marriage.

I don't know who is sitting to the right or left of my parents; these parts of the photo have been cut away. Somehow, this is fitting. My father was supposed to marry Greek, and his break with tradition set our family apart.

### Flashback

The Sweet Shop, Oyster Bay, Long Island. My mostly Irish American mother in a booth with her twin sister, Patsy, sipping an egg cream, made by my father, who is smitten. My mother is amused by his broken English, jet-black hair greased into a ducktail. After my father's shift is over, they go on a double date: John and Nancy, Patsy and Jim. Bowling or a movie.

Gus, my father's older brother, bangs on the door of my mother's home on Summers Street later that evening. He drags my father out to the sidewalk, where they get into a fistfight. But it's no use. My parents are in love.

### The Girls

My parents have been married just shy of two years when my sister Paulette is born. I follow fifteen months later. Suzanne is born two years after me, and Georgia fifteen months after her. Each time, my father prays for a boy. My parents stop trying at four and name my youngest sister for my father's father, as a gesture. In Greece, the first-born son is named for his paternal grandfather.

### Fast Forward

A decade after Georgia is born, my mother gives birth to a boy. He lies in the nursery, tightly swaddled, his fat red head poking out from the blanket. At ten pounds, two-and-a-half ounces, he is almost twice the size of the other newborns in the nursery, and nameless for two days. My father must have thought a son wasn't in the stars for him. Eight months prior to this day, my mother had bequeathed the naming to us girls, and our father did not protest. Now, we stand in a circle, giving in to our father one by one as he pleads with us to name my brother George instead of Brian.

A month before George Brian turns three, my mother gives birth to a second boy, Michael John, and our family is complete.

### The Pettit Sisters

My mother has six sisters: Ellen, Patsy, Margie, Josephine, Maisie, and Frances. We sit around a table, drinking tea with milk and sugar and eating Irish soda bread, buttered. My sisters are off to the side, playing. (This is before the boys.) I am glued to the conversation, always a lover of story.

They laugh about the time my mother and my aunts Patsy and Margie tried to get into a high school dance for free through the girls' bathroom window, failing because they laughed so hard that one of my aunts peed her pants.

Then stories about my grandfather, who bought a bag of liquor for himself and a bag of candy for his kids on payday. They called him Fred and dropped pennies on his head from the second-floor window. Some nights, he passed out on the grate in the kitchen floor, above the coal furnace.

Finally, one of my favorites, the story about the big switch. I can picture my mother and her twin puffing on stale smokes from the pack that they kept hidden under a bench, laughing about fooling the nuns. My mother excelled in math and my aunt Patsy in English so they sometimes took tests for the other, indistinguishable in their Catholic schoolgirl uniforms.

I can see, hear, taste, and touch these stories. I can easily imagine myself in their world, and often do.

Sometimes my grandmother, who emigrated from Ireland to take care of rich ladies and their children, joins us for tea. She is usually at the Cuttings', where she returned to work after her eldest children were old enough to look after the youngest. My mother has a brother, too, Martin.

## The Greeks

This is how my mother refers to my father's side of the family. At The Greeks', my sisters and I are praised for our good manners. We sit quietly, eating *kourabiéthes*, butter cookies covered in powdered sugar, and *melomakárona*, spiced cookies soaked in honey and covered with crushed walnuts. The grownups, except for my mother, sip thick coffee from demitasse cups.

My father's family reminisces about their lives in Skoura, Lakonia, Greece, a small agrarian village on the Peloponnese, but they do so in Greek, a language both wholly familiar to me and completely out of reach. At some point during the conversation, my father or one of his siblings translates for us.

My father and his brothers took turns camping out in the lookout for days in the middle of the olive fields, watching for fires.

When their youngest brother broke his leg, a woman in the village moved the bones back into place; she had the cult of a witch doctor.

They loaded up donkeys and horses with containers of olives, oil, lemons, and oranges to sell at the market in Sparta, thirteen kilometers away.

My aunts, along with other children from the villages, were sent to feeding camps after World War II, where they were fed five times a day to fatten them back up.

The family came over by boat in ones, twos, and threes. Gus, the eldest, immigrated in 1951; his father and sister Georgia in 1955; my father, three months shy of his twenty-first birthday, in May 1958. His mother, younger brother, Louie, and youngest sister, Paula, followed in September.

They joined my great-grandfather, who had immigrated in 1910 with his brothers and cousins. Their wives and children were to follow once there was enough money to send for them. My great-grandfather's wife and children never did. This is how that story goes:

My great-grandmother's cousin, who patrolled the olive fields, which were sometimes plundered by gypsies, came to my great-grandmother's home for coffee. As he was lifting his rifle, which hung from a strap on his shoulder, he accidentally shot and killed her. My grandfather, who was only a year old, remained in the village and was raised, along with his older sister, by his grandmother, who was blind.

These stories sound like Grimm's fairy tales, and the start-and-stop way in which they unfold creates a distance that I am unable to traverse.

When we children are excused from the table, we beg our cousins to speak English, to which Soula, the youngest of her family, responds, "English, English!" It isn't her fault that she is just learning the language, in kindergarten. Her brothers, Peter and George, who have mastered English by now, are used to speaking Greek at home.

I envy my cousins for their ability to live in both worlds and get lost in neither.

### The Diner

My mother, my sisters, and I sit in the big booth in the back of the Colony Diner. The jukebox has been rigged to play 45s for free. We're privy to the trick since my father, his brother Gus, and their brother-in-law John own the place.

We study the menus: thick as books and impossible to memorize. Every day there are specials, and breakfast is served anytime. There are sections for burgers, sandwiches, salads, steaks and chops, seafood, Italian fare, Greek specials, and beverages, which come soft, hot, and hard. Bakery cases are filled with cream pies, fruit pies, cheesecakes, napoleons, éclairs, and fruit tarts, and the counter is lined with giant chocolate chip cookies, linzer tortes, Danishes, muffins, brownies, and *ruggelah*, a Russian-Jewish treat.

My father and uncles are off to the side, with red faces and raised voices. My mother doesn't mind not knowing what they say; in fact, she takes delight in saying, "It's all Greek to me."

**Night Shift**

When we get home from school, my father is just waking up. He stands at the top of the stairs in his underwear, with sleepy hair, a bit disoriented. Then he sits in front of the TV with a bowl of Kellogg's Corn Flakes, watching Luke and Laura on *General Hospital*, his prelude to a night of work.

For dinner, my sisters and I will have Campbell's tomato soup and grilled cheese sandwiches, one of our mother's specialties. Or she'll spirit us away to McDonald's to eat what my father refers to as horse meat.

In the morning, my sisters and I awaken to our favorite diner pastries, packs of gum, and rolls of Life Savers—gifts from our father, who climbed into bed a few hours before. I quietly cut into my cheese Danish, pop a spearmint Life Saver into my mouth, and hide my pack of orange Trident in my dresser drawer.

**Day Shift**

My sisters and I climb out of the aboveground swimming pool in our backyard, where we've turned pruny playing *Jaws* and swimming around and around to make whirlpools. The back door and windows of our house are shut tight to preserve the air-conditioned climate. Our mother is in the basement, folding laundry. Our father is just about to get up from the plastic-covered faux-velvet couch—modern Greek American style—to cook dinner. He's been relaxing to Poly Panou, his favorite Greek singer, after being on his feet all day.

I make a silent wish for broiled chicken with french fries, and not *fasolákia*, the stew of green beans, zucchini, eggplant, potato, and tomato that reminds him of home.

**Summer of '75**

A black-and-white photo: sun spot in the left-hand corner, then my sister Paulette, who is almost as tall as my mother in her platform shoes; my mother, with dark, round sunglasses, short hair; my father with a slight pompadour, black-and-white patent leather shoes; then me in flowered culottes, standing between my father and a headless, half-armed goddess. Suzanne and Georgia stand in front of my father and mother in white kneesocks and sandals, same as me.

We are in the garden outside the museum in Sparta, being photographed by a man with an old-fashioned camera. He hides behind a curtain, snaps the shot, and then develops it right there.

Being in Greece is like traveling back in time. The only TV in Skoura is at my grandparents' house, and it is a black-and-white set. The only car belongs to the village doctor. Everyone else gets around by foot, donkey, tractor, bus, or taxi.

My sisters and I drink a lot of Coca-Cola, which we buy at the *magazí*, the village store. There is plenty of fresh fruit in the village, but no juice. The only milk is goat's milk. I run from the table when I learn that we are eating rabbit, and not just any rabbit, but the one I had befriended who used to live in the cage outside. I soak a pillow with tears while my family finishes the meal. My sisters say it tasted like chicken.

Now we are vacationing by the Mediterranean, a sea-sized pool. We stay in a hotel owned by relatives. Our room has four metal beds covered with sheets, no spreads. The floor, walls, and ceiling, where lizards nap, are made of concrete. Down the hall there are American toilets in individual shacks with fifty-gallon drums of water and buckets, in lieu of plumbing.

In the sea, I hold on to my father's back when I grow tired, the beach barely visible as we swim our way toward a sandbar. When we reach it, we wave furiously back at my mother, who is growing crisp on the sand and, no doubt, can't see us.

Back in Skoura, we pile into the hitch on a tractor, equipped with a table and chairs, and drive to the next village, on the other side of the olive groves. We sit at our table, surrounded by tables and chairs from other tractors, eating roast pork from a pig that rotates above a spit. My sisters and I get up with our father to dance, joining a circle of dancers looping around other circles of dancers. I can see my mother, sitting at the table, thoroughly amused by her four daughters, who are busy tripping over their feet.

The night before our departure, it seems as if the entire village comes by to bid us farewell, downing shots of ouzo and smashing their glasses on the floor, "*Kaló taxithí,*" literally translated "good journey."

Widows dressed in black pull me into their laps, pinching my neck and grazing the fat of my arm with their teeth. I can see my mother, in the bedroom with my sisters, laughing. Nobody seems to mind that she usually breaks off from the adults and goes away with her girls, freed from the indiscernible chatter. We are five females who can only manage "*Yeia sou, ti káneis?*" and "*Kalá, kai esí?*" ("Hello, how are you?" "Fine, and you?")

**Fast Forward**

A black-and-white photo, no sun spot. Me in a flowered, sleeveless blouse, Birkenstock sandals, my arm around my cousin Yiota, who wears a white shirt and dark shorts. We are in the garden outside the museum in Sparta, and the same man who stood behind the curtain of his camera in 1975 is behind it now.

**Summer of '87**

I fly to Greece on my own, take a taxi from the airport to the bus station, a bus from Athens to Sparta, and then a taxi from Sparta to Skoura. When the taxi arrives in the village square, I freeze. There are no addresses for houses, so I say our family name to the driver, using the Greek pronunciation. "Foondás." I remember that my grandparents' house is close to the church, so I look up the word in my English-Greek dictionary. "*Ekklesía.*" The taxi driver pulls up to a house near the church where a bunch of women are sitting on the porch. One of these women is my grandmother. When she sees me climb out of the taxi, she starts to cry. Yiayia says something in Greek as she hugs me close and strokes my hair. My cousin Yiota, who is learning English in school, translates: "We thought you were coming tomorrow."

"*Páme yia vólta.*" ("Let's go for a walk.") I feel like a child, trailing Yiota through the village. She is twelve; I am twenty-three. But we become fast friends, pointing to objects as we go, exchanging Greek for English and English for Greek.

Every evening, Yiota and I walk to the village cemetery to float a wick in olive oil at the head of my grandfather's grave. In four years, his flesh will have fully decomposed and his bones will be exhumed. Land is precious in Greek villages.

Pappou died in 1984. The last time I saw him, he was in a hospital in New York receiving chemotherapy treatments. The family had flown him over from Greece in hopes of preserving his life. The day I visited him, my Greek relatives lined the perimeter of the room, engrossed in conversation. I sat by Pappou's bed and held his hand, my only means of communication. Now, I can feel him by my side.

## A Day's Routine

In the morning, I awaken to the clatter of coffee-making in the kitchen. When Yiayia is done with her breakfast, she sits outside to *pléko*, turning cotton thread into a delicate doily using a small crochet hook. I join her with a cup of tea, a novel, my journal, postcards, and stationery. Not used to being so silent, I read and write half the day away.

At about ten o'clock, Yiayia picks vegetables from her garden, then disappears into the *mageireió*, a one-room kitchen made of concrete blocks and detached from the house. This is where she cooks the main meal. It is equipped with a propane stove top, a fifty-gallon drum of olive oil, and a cast iron stove. Pots and pans, a cheese grater, and a colander hang on the walls.

We eat vegetable dishes or fish on Mondays, Wednesdays, Fridays, and Saturdays. Lamb on Sundays, roasted in the oven in the indoor kitchen. And chicken or pork chops on Tuesdays and Thursdays. Some days, Yiayia fills the cast iron stove with small logs that cook down to charcoal, which she transports to the grill with a metal dustpan. Stray cats gather outside the gates as the chicken sizzles and spits above the flames. Potatoes fried in olive oil and a tomato salad accompany the meat.

Yiayia and I eat in awkward silence at noon. My favorite village fare is *vleeta*, a bowl of Greek greens with the fruit, leaf, and flower from a zucchini plant. We dip thick slices of peasant bread into the broth, and I smile.

After the meal, I wash the dishes, and once a week, Yiayia washes her hair. I watch as she unwinds the braids that sit on top of her head. She washes her crimped hair in the same deep sink where she soaks our underwear in bleach water or quarters a chicken. Then she sits in the sun and combs it out. She parts her hair in two, and braids each side, adding a black ribbon toward the end. She pulls the braids on top of her head and secures them in place by tying the ends of the ribbons together. Then she covers most of her hair with a black cap, crocheted by her hands. I gather the gray and white strands that came free and wrap them up in paper—a keepsake.

Between two and four o'clock, the entire village rests. The men have already come in from the olive fields to eat; the women are finished cleaning up from the meal; the two *kafenio* and *magazi* close their doors to business. Most of the village sleeps, including Yiayia, but I'm not attuned to this midday nap, so I sit outside and listen to the silence. Donkeys bray to one another throughout the village. Chickens cluck. Goats bleat. I can hear the buzz of bees. And I feel like I've come home.

## Fast Forward

I am sitting at a table in the dining room of the Colony, surrounded by The Greeks. It is October 1991, and I have just returned from my second solo trip to Skoura, a four-month stay. I took beginning and intermediate Greek before going. This time, I filled fewer journals and wrote home far less. And I started my first fictions, inspired by inhabitants of the village.

I also learned to *plekó*. Every morning, Yiayia and I sat side by side, her hands moving confidently, mine slowly, often having to undo work when I missed a double loop. While our hands moved, I listened to Yiayia's stories.

The day I left, Yiayia slipped a gold ring from her finger, engraved with the letters **ΑΦ**, and enclosed it in the palm of my hand. I am Angelikoúla—little Angela—her namesake.

Here, back in the States, I listen to my aunts and uncles gossiping, in Greek, about other Greeks, the waitresses, their children. I smile and nod and laugh, sipping coffee.

## Flashback

A moving picture, in color. I stand at the foot of Pappou's grave; Yiayia sits opposite me, wailing. Male relatives take turns digging down to the pine casket. When my uncle hits wood, he uses his hands to brush away the earth. The white sheet that covered Pappou's body when he was buried is pulled aside, revealing a skull—the color of red clay—poking from a suit. This is taken up first. Then shoulders, arms, hands, ribs. Pelvis, thighs, shins. Each foot gently shaken from its sock. Then the women wash them all. When the gold tooth is pulled from his skull, I hold out my hand.

# LONE STARS

## Lan Tran

I AM DRESSED LIKE TEXAS. It is past my bedtime but I am moon-struck with the idea of being a cowgirl—after all, we live in the Lone Star State. There I am, slant eyes and a longhorn drawl, bowl-cut hair and a ten-gallon hat. I have converted my jump rope into a lasso. It hangs awkwardly around my waist. I stomp my rodeo boots and sing at my father:

> The stars at night are big and bright,
> Deep in the heart of Texas!

I go for volume, not melody. He is silent, as if he does not recognize me. I evolve from rice paddy to cow patty with this entire campfire repertoire from school, which I trot out every evening. Though I push him to, my father does not sing along. Yellow is for skin, not roses.

"*Di ngu di,*" ("Go to bed.") he says, turning away.

"Aren't you going to clap?"

This is our nightly ritual. We are more than an ocean apart.


One night when I am five, my father does acknowledge me, even though we have guests. My mother is still at work when he says, "Little One, bring out the *tra*, then you can go play." He gestures at a large teapot filled with a dark herbal drink. It smells of pretty blossoms and earthy roots, but I make a sour face because I am painfully shy around strangers. Our living room is packed with Vietnamese college students who have come to hear my father discuss politics.

"Go," my father says, handing me a tray. I walk into the living room first, but he quickly moves around me to go to his seat. Everyone is focused on my father's words when he begins to speak. Before them he is another person. Though dressed plainly, as always, in brown pants and a simple white shirt, there is a charisma about him I do not often see. "We are not economic immigrants," he tells his audience. "We are political refugees." The students nod, listening raptly. My movements are an intrusion, so I nervously set the tray down and scurry back to the warmth of the kitchen. Behind me, my father's voice echoes, "We must remember our history."

History, I nod to myself, thinking of my homework. At school, we are learning about our proud Texan heritage and our assignment is to draw pictures reflecting that pride. In addition, we have been promised extra-credit stars if we bring in special projects. I have already earned a spangling row next to my name. I am a shameless hoarder of stars.

The previous night, I folded a paper pony for class. My teacher was charmed, so tonight I am determined to outdo myself. I am going to make a chuck wagon!

I take out a white sheet of paper, making careful folds to ensure the creases are sharp and precise. Through the door, I hear my father say, "We have lost our homeland and are marooned in a foreign country."

I sit, assessing my wagon. It needs something more. In the other room, my father is saying, "Until there is no more communism, there is no home to return to." A murmur rises from the students, the significance of which escapes me. Whenever I have asked my mother, "Why do these people have to come over and listen to Dad?" I have been told he has very important ideas. But it is all vague to me; the only thing I know is that Vietnam is extremely important to my father.

Vietnam . . . yes! I have the perfect idea for my chuck wagon project! Something to please both my teacher and my dad. I grab the red and yellow markers nearby and with a few quick strokes, I color the wagon's covering so it looks like the Vietnamese flag in my classroom atlas.

Now, I know the mini nylon banner on my father's desk looks different than the flag in the atlas—his flag is yellow, like our coloring, with three red horizontal stripes representing the lifeblood of Vietnam's northern, central, and southern regions. But the nylon banner is old, and I learned at school that flags can change. We Texans haven't always flown our current colors: red, white, and blue with a single star. During the Texas revolution, a white cotton flag was unfurled, with a black cannon and the words COME AND TAKE IT painted beneath. Naturally, I want my project to have the most up-to-date emblem of my father's homeland. I want to make something unforgettable.

When I finish coloring my special project, I continue drawing more pictures for school. A little later, my father comes in for more *tra*. "Are you having a good talk, Daddy?" He grunts to indicate its acceptability. "What are you talking about?" I ask him.

"*Chinh tri ve dat nuoc. Con chua hieu duoc,*" ("Political matters, our national landscape. You're too young to understand.") he answers.

"I know landscape," I protest, then show him my drawing of a cactus in the sun. "And look," I find another picture, "this is Texas." I hand him a purple outline of my beloved land.

My father regards the dark lines meant to convey the edges and boundaries of my home state. *"Nhung con co biet ve Viet Nam khong?"* ("But can you draw Vietnam?") he asks. I hold an uncapped marker in my right hand, hesitant. Is he really asking me to draw it? Though I have memorized the shape of Texas, the borders of Vietnam are hazy.

*"Yeu nuoc nhu vay,"* ("You're quite a patriot.") my father chides.

"I am a patriot," I say.

My father shakes his head, a certain gesture of his disappointment.

*"Con nghi con hieu long ai quoc?"* ("You think you know patriotism?")

I nod vigorously at first, remembering a recent field trip to the Alamo—our tour around the famous mission, we children wide-eyed at the stone church, the wooden barracks. And oh, the gift shop with the armadillo toys!

"Davy Crockett was a patriot," I say.

*"Con dau co biet."* ("You have no idea what it means.") *"Ong noi con yeu nuoc,"* ("Your grandfather was a patriot.") he corrects me. He wags his finger slowly and deliberately—a wiper that sweeps my confidence away. *"Con khong biet Vietnam."* ("You don't know Vietnam.")

I clench my fists, steaming. This is my father, a man to whom I can never give the right answers, to whom I am wrong because I am not Vietnamese enough.

When he turns his back, my eye catches the colored wagon beneath the other drawings. Maybe this will please him. While he gets more hot water, I lift the top napkin from the tea tray and place my chuck wagon beneath it. Moments later, my father carries the tray into the other room. I listen for sounds of approval, but instead I hear the tray slamming down and my name being yelled.

I walk into the living room slowly. There is a pool of liquid on the table where the tea has spilled, but my father is focused on something else.

"Little One, did you draw this?" He holds up the chuck wagon—two of its wheels are soggy but it has the blood red covering I colored and is emblazoned with a lone star: golden, big, and bright. Everywhere I look, unfriendly eyes stare at me. I nod.

"Why?"

"Because it's the flag of Vietnam." There is a dark mumbling among the visitors, and they look at each other.

My father slams his palm on the coffee table, then lifts the chuck wagon higher, shaking it. *"Day la co cong san, con ve co giet hai nuoc!"* ("This is the flag of communist Vietnam! You have drawn the flag that murdered our homeland!") He points to the golden star. "This is *not* our flag!"

My father rips my chuck wagon in half. I am dismissed. The meeting ends.

In the silence of my room, I kick the wall. My sharp-toed boots leave a faint mark, which I bend to wipe off and then decide not to. Though my father's words incite deep longing in others—a vision of Vietnam free from communists—what I hear incites anger and shame in me. I am an activist's daughter, but from that moment on, I actively remain ignorant of his causes. For many years, I care more about Sam Houston than Saigon. I remember the Alamo. My father remembers Vietnam.


Three words. Dien Bien Phu. I am a college student when these words come for me, a mouthful of reprimand. In the dorms to let off steam during midterms, we are playing "Jeopardy" in teams. There are five of us on each team and the tie-breaking answer is, "In 1954, the French lost a major battle here to the Viet Minh. This led to the north-south partition of Vietnam along the 17th parallel."

My teammates cannot believe our luck. A Vietnamese history question! They don't even bother conferring, just hand me a fat felt pen to write down our answer. Someone pats me on the back.

Across from us, the other team is deep in a huddle, whispering and glancing at me nervously. They think I am speechless because I know the answer. The only thing I know is that the northern part went to the communists. "Hurry," a teammate whispers, "we're gonna kick some ass!" I write down "What is the DMZ?" because I once heard a Vietnam vet say he traveled there.

The other team's card reads, "What is Dien Bien Phu?" The winners jump up and down. My teammates stare at me openmouthed in disbelief.

"What the hell's wrong with you?" one of them finally asks.

I want to say, "Hey, I'm American," but I don't know anything about the U.S. in Vietnam either, except what I've seen in movies.


"You were five years old when a *what* traumatized you?"

I'm with my roommate, who's an editor for our school's African American paper, trying to explain why I'm not as in touch with my roots as she is.

"A chuck wagon," I mumble.

"A what?"

I thought she would be understanding, but the more I try to explain to her—

"A chuck wagon."

"How old are you?"

—the more I'm beginning to realize how foolish it all seems.

"I'm twenty."

"Exactly. That happened almost fifteen years ago. Don't you think it's time to let it go?" I just fidget, so she says, "I mean, my parents piss me off, too, but you don't see me tryin' to stop being black." When I don't respond, she shakes her head. "A chuck wagon."

Perhaps my grievance is outweighed by my ignorance.


"Dad, what happened in Vietnam?" It is winter break, months later, and I am home for the holidays.

"Happened when?" We are eating dinner together, and he does not look at me as he reaches for pieces of stuffed bitter melon.

"I don't know," I shrug, "how about the twentieth century?" There, I've admitted my ignorance; now he will be really annoyed. But he looks up, stops chewing, and then points his chopsticks at me and says, "Come with me."

"But we're eating . . ."

"It's more important," my father taps his temple, "that you consume this."

I follow him into the family room and watch as he roots around inside a tall, dark cabinet to bring out an old map of Vietnam. It crinkles with history as he unfolds it. The map is so old, a colonial relic, that our country is labeled *Indochine*.

"Here," my father points at an ambiguous landmass. "This is where the Chinese invaded centuries ago. And here," he indicates another region, "is where the French came in centuries later."

As we sit on the wool rug, I am struck by my father's patience. I thought he would be appalled at my ignorance—there were all those times as a child when he dismissed me with condescension. But tonight, it is as if he's been expecting my questions—has been expecting them for quite some time. "During the French occupation, my family and I had to dig a tunnel under our property and live there. One day, they torched our house. We sat beneath in the darkness, listening to the sounds of our home burning down. It was incredibly hot." He speaks slowly, but my mind races to capture all the details.

My father then narrates a timeline and, as he progresses, the names of historical figures begin bleeding into names of family. With each major battle, my father also recounts the death of one of our kin. "In the 1954 campaign against the French, your great uncle died," he says, or, "During a battle in '67 they bombed my cousin's school, killing him." I have never met these people; they are brittle leaves on our family tree, so at the mention of each name I ask, "Did you know him well?" or, "Were you close to him?"

My father nods vaguely each time and continues to describe a litany of events, each tied to another name and another and another until the distance between the past and present dissolves as each death draws closer and closer to my dad. From ancestor to great-grandfather to grandfather to his generation, at times he must grit his teeth to continue handing me this history of Vietnam: a heartbreaking tally of men he has known and loved. There are moments when I do not recognize the quaver in his voice. When he finishes, I am speechless. We do not look at each other, just stare at the map—its intimate curves indicating landmasses and waterways. If we could cry together, there would be tears enough to wash all the borders between the Alamo and Dien Bien Phu.

"There is something you should know . . . about your grandfather's death."

"How he fell? The train? Mom said it was a horrible accident."

"Well, he did fall, but it was no accident."

"Someone pushed him? Mom said—"

"Little One, your mother doesn't know this. Your grandfather originally fought with the Viet Minh for a free Vietnam but wanted to leave them when they unveiled their communist agenda. He thought he'd be safe in Hanoi, but they still went after him for 'crimes against the people.'"

"Even though he once fought with them?"

My father nods. "Your grandfather knew the communists were determined to find him guilty—which would also condemn his children—so for our freedom, he chose to kill himself. But, he couldn't commit suicide outright, since that would be admitting guilt, so he faked it. It looked accidental, but your grandfather jumped to his death for your aunts, your uncle . . . and for me."

My father now tears openly. I do not ask, "Were you close to him?" Instead I watch his hand trace the 17th parallel on the map, and I think of the imaginary line my grandfather crossed when he stepped off the platform. Instinctively my hand trails my father's and we brush over mountains and rivers as our fingers sweep, mine following his, across the page. Suddenly, my father stops. Why, I am uncertain. But as my hand approaches his, he reaches for mine. And when I look at him, he squeezes.

They say, too, that at the Alamo, when they knew they were outnumbered, Colonel Travis drew a line in the sand and said, "Anyone who's willing to die, cross this line!"

# SAYING SOMETHING IN AFRICAN

### Emiene Shija Wright

EMIENE: NO PLAN SUCCEEDS WITHOUT GOD.

Shija: Come, let us go.

I used to wonder why my parents gave me these names. To me, these were warrior names, names for people who would face trials and uncertainty. In this light, my name was almost prophetic—but the biggest struggle I faced growing up was becoming comfortable in my own self.

Jos, Nigeria, mid-1970s. An African American woman lies in a hospital bed, hoping she has made the right decision to have this child. She has not been home in almost a decade, and her marriage is on the rocks. From the window, she looks out over the courtyard, and sees a dog loping across it with a human placenta in his mouth. Right then, her water breaks.

I was born to an African American mother and a Nigerian father. My mother taught at a school for girls, and my father was a bureaucrat within the police department. For the first half of my childhood, my home was part of a large compound in the village of Adikpo. Despite the kerosene generator, it was a fairly modern house with a sunken living room, piano, and our own bedrooms. My grandfather, Buono, his two wives and children, my uncle and his family, my parents, my brother and two sisters, and three servants all lived together in the compound. Each family had a separate dwelling that faced the common yard. My parents ran a restaurant with rooms for rent in one of the unoccupied buildings, and my aunt and her family were frequent visitors. My home was filled with people, and I was the baby of them all.

Every morning, Uncle Tion came by for our walk. He would be angry if my mother didn't have me dressed and ready to go. I would ride on his shoulders to the local bar, and we would tarry for hours gossiping with neighbors and friends. After enough "hot drinks," someone was sure to slip me a few sips and then I would be tipsy, too, which amused Tion no end. It was our secret, and one of the reasons he was my favorite uncle. In the afternoon, my siblings and I biked around the village. I refused to ride with my oldest sister, who in my opinion could ride only slightly better than I could, opting instead for my big brother's handlebars. We made a lot of good-natured mischief, from stealing cigarettes to spying on local politicians staying overnight with their mistresses. When it rained, we would play in the downpour while the adults put out receptacles to catch the water. In good times, a party at our home could last several days.

My mother and I conversed in English, but I spoke with a British accent, the way most English-speakers around me did. She never learned to speak Tiv, my father's ethnic language, very well. I didn't mind. I spoke Tiv with my dad, and didn't like it when my mother tried to join in. "That's our language," I would say in my four-year-old lisp. It was a rare intimacy between me and my dad, and I guarded it jealously.

Even as a young child, I got on with my father poorly. His middle daughter, a robust, active child, was his favorite. She was a fast runner, and could kick a soccer ball like a boy. I, on the other hand, was more introverted and shy. She loved for him to swing her through the air by her arms, but whenever he tried this with me, I invariably ended up with a bump on the head. His mustache always seemed to scratch my face when he kissed me, and his hands were harder than my mother's when he spanked me. But I was hungry for his attention. So I spoke Tiv, and when he and my mother argued, as they did often, I broke things on purpose. I blamed him for the strife, since when he was away things were peaceful. He in turn said my mother must have had bad thoughts about him when I was in her belly, and stopped swinging me through the air.

My mother was industrious and generally liked in the community. Having a restaurant/inn on the premises was her idea, and it was profitable. She was given the name Hemba Don, Glorious One, by my grandfather Buono. Their relationship was more affectionate than he and my father's. Buono was a respected elder known for making powerful medicines. He and my mother were both early risers, and he compared her favorably with the other women in the compound. "Look at this," he would say, "Hemba Don has dressed the children, made me breakfast, and been to the market already, and you people are still about yawning and scratching your bottoms-o. Ah-ah!"

Though good-looking, my father was not so well liked. His mother, Bueh, was a junior wife, younger, and under the authority of Buono's earlier, more established wives. She produced only two children, my father and my aunt, another blow to their status in the household. As a youngster, he had to bribe the other kids with kola nuts to play with him—but those days were long behind him. By the time he and my mother met, he was a sophisticated man of the world. He had been educated in British schools and was a very stylish dresser. He drove luxury cars, shunned palm wine for imported Italian, and listened mainly to classical music. My father loved going out to clubs and parties, despite being an awful dancer. His real talent lay in impressing women. On their first date, he surprised my mother with a dress and a pair of shoes that fit her perfectly, without having to ask her size. They married less than six months later. It was a case of opposites attracting. Unfortunately, it didn't work.

Politically, the two were as different as night and day. My mother was a fierce idealist. In the States, she had been active in the protest movement, and studied nonviolent resistance. But seeing police dogs attack Southern children and the murder of Malcolm X, she sheared off her straightened hair and booked a flight on the first thing smoking to West Africa. She landed with a bachelor's degree and a friend's address in her pocket. She was probably more in love with Africa than with my dad. My father, on the other hand, was a budding conservative. He was scornful of those who weren't educated, including members of his own family.

My father's carefully cultivated manners hid a nasty surprise: self-hate. Though he would not explicitly admit it, he believed Europeans superior to Africans in almost every way. "Look at that," he would say of his half-brother Gbayo, a beautiful dark boy our age with whom we often played, "the black sheep amongst the white." Upon learning of her membership in the Urban League, he accused my mother of plotting to overthrow the U.S. government, despite the league's reputation for being more moderate than the NAACP.

Their fights were epic and stingingly personal. "I do not want my children knowing that their mother descended from slaves!" he raged when she taught us American history. "Why not?" she replied. "Your people did the selling." Every so often, women my father said were "crazy" would show up at our door, shouting at him, or they would send angry letters in the mail. Some women were Nigerian, some African American, and once there was even a schoolgirl. I was not allowed to read the letters, but I guessed at their contents, because my mother reacted to the letters the same way she did after a visit—she would shake her head and laugh quietly to herself, all day long. But she looked like she wanted to cry.

Montgomery, Alabama, mid-1980s. After nine years, my parents divorced, and my mother returned with us children to her home in Alabama. Her mother had recently died, and my mother was too drained to fight the child-support settlement—an astonishing $150 a month for four children. She had been outside Alabama's social and political network for fifteen years, so even though she had risen to the level of principal in Africa, finding teaching work was difficult.

Mom took a night job, and sold Avon products out of a small grocery store on the side. We kids sold penny candy at school and cups of frozen Kool-Aid in the neighborhood during summer. Our clothes, though clean and neat, were never the latest styles, and when the car stopped working, there was no money to have it fixed. We simply took the bus and budgeted within an inch of our lives. Despite hardship, we had a close-knit family, and went to museums, patronized the library, and performed in a local children's theater my mother started. We had a lot of good times together.

At first, I was not used to seeing so many white people, and I thought something was wrong with them. "Oh Mommy," I said, upon seeing a popular shampoo commercial in which a woman repeatedly tossed her head, "what happened to that lady's hair? It's so messy! She can't even braid it!"

I attended a Catholic school on a need-based scholarship. Although it was an excellent private school, oftentimes I found myself speaking an English superior to that of my instructors. The kids were another story altogether. There is no place in Alabama for a little black girl with a British accent. It was as though I had dropped from the sky.

"Say something in African!" At recess, I was regularly swarmed by dozens of kids, all with this same demand. It baffled me. To them, Africa was one big jungle, not a continent broken up by thousands of languages. They laughed when I used British terms—referring to a car trunk as "the boot" and to french fries as "chips"—and when I didn't understand slang. Though I knew their behavior was more curious than malicious, I became very shy and self-conscious, and tried hard to lose my accent so I wouldn't feel so different from everyone.

Eventually, even the reduced tuition became too much of a burden, and I had to switch to public school. Not to be surmounted, my mother made provisions for me to participate in the "M-and-M" program, so called because it provided buses to transport kids from all-black neighborhoods to magnet schools across town, in mostly white areas. Again I stood out because of my accent and almost Victorian manners. I was tipped for gifted programs, and I excelled almost effortlessly. For some reason, these novelties enraged my new classmates.

Monkey. Tarzan. African booty-scratcher. I was called these names every day for the next four years. Although the school was predominantly white, the African American students were the ones who persecuted me relentlessly. The dark-skinned kids were especially cruel, quickest to disparage my African ancestry. My pointing out that they were darker than me was the quickest route to a fight. I learned to ignore the gaps around me in line, to avoid groups of unsupervised kids in the halls, and to stay in the bathroom until lunchtime was almost over. Generally my tormenters had to settle for sneaking pushes, handling my homework between pinched fingers, and pretending that I stank. They behaved as though being African were a disease they did not want to catch.

Even by the late 1980s, most of the students' concepts of Africa were based on old Tarzan movies and images of starving Ethiopian children. They had a deep-seated hostility toward anything African. "I'm not black, I'm brown," the kids would say. During Black History Month, when images of dancing Africans wearing fringe and playing drums were shown, they were palpably embarrassed. These pictures, which featured dancers in unusual and grotesque contortions, took the Africans out of a cultural context and seemed designed to engender feelings of shame in black kids. The taunting was a little more pointed those days. The images contradicted the reality before them of a high-achieving, well-spoken African. Cognitive dissonance showed on their faces: Either they had been lied to about Africa or I was putting on an elaborate front to hide my true uncivilized nature. The depth of their anger suggests they believed the latter.

Despite the bullying, I clung to the belief that it was they who had the problem, not me. "Hey girl, is you a African?" "Yes," I would reply to hoots of laughter. The constant tormenting drummed into me that I was different. I was African. A defiant pride became my shield. The more I was called an African in epithet, the more obligated I felt to excel and contradict the notions of what an African was supposed to be.

One day on the playground, everything spun out of control. It started no different from any other recess: I was the last one picked, and my team was angry to get stuck with me. I think I missed a ball. My teacher, who regularly turned a blind eye to the abuse, found me surrounded by a ring of kids yelling, shoving, and kicking me. I was crying but fighting back. She scolded all of us, but asked only me to stay after class. "Why are you always the center of attention, Emiene? Why is everyone always picking on you?"

I considered her question. Since transferring to the school, I had done my best to avoid trouble. I got straight As, or the rare B in math. I hardly spoke to anyone, and I had only one friend, who was not in any of my classes. My throat tightened with the effort of holding back tears. There could be only one explanation. "Because I'm African." She looked at me for a long time with an impassive expression. Tears started rolling down my face. "Well," she said, "you'll just have to try harder to get along."

At home, my mother tried to keep me connected to my heritage, but it was difficult for her, since she wasn't Nigerian herself. She taught me to cook Nigerian dishes and attempted to transmit cultural knowledge based on her own experiences, but something within me started to change. I began tuning her out. Going to Africa had been the greatest adventure of her life, and at times it seemed Africa was the only thing my mother wanted to talk about. She introduced my siblings and me to strangers as her "African children."

More than anything the kids at school said, my mother's behavior embarrassed me. It was bad enough that others slapped "African" on my forehead to avoid seeing me as a person. It felt as though my mother was doing the same thing, though with a positive spin. More than anything, I just wanted to be allowed to be, the way it seemed other people just were.

I lost fluency in Tiv, since I saw my father only during vacations and we spoke English exclusively by then. Strangely, my mother began using Tiv with me in front of others. Perhaps she wanted to keep me connected, but it felt so unnatural—we still never spoke it in private. I felt like she was showing off, trotting me out like an exotic dog or life-size souvenir. I quietly rebelled by acting as though I couldn't understand her, or using the most substandard English I could muster. I was American, too, African American like her, and I refused to "say something in African" so she could set me apart.

In spite of my distaste for my mother's nostalgia for Africa, by junior high I too began exploiting my connection. I was shy, so it helped to be known for something other than nerdy good grades. I was known as "the girl from Africa," and I was popular. I learned to spin my story into something exotic and cool, dropping details that implied our servants were the starched and ironed type, not the barefoot, dusty houseboys that we treated like family. I was a fraud, but I rationalized my behavior, thinking it was about time being African actually benefited me somehow. I looked forward to college, and the day I would meet "people like me," people to whom the label "African" would not be a blessing or a curse, but simply a part of who I was.

I met other Africans my age for the first time at college in Michigan. Though I had some male friends who were African, the majority of my friends were African American. Still, I attended meetings of the African Student Union. I wanted to belong so badly I did the thing I'd hated the most: I fetishized them, seeing the African students as a group I wanted to belong to, rather than as individuals.

Sometimes I even found myself speaking with an accent I didn't possess. It broke my heart to hear the affectionate *o* caressing the ends of sentences, which I had nearly forgotten since moving away from my extended family. I couldn't resist adding it myself, and repeating, however slightly, their melodic cadence in my own speech. That quickly stopped when a few students broke into a round of Yoruba with me, and wanted to know why I couldn't respond. When pressed for details, it felt like an apology to say that my parents were divorced and I had been raised by my African American mother. I didn't want pity, I wanted acceptance. But my lack of cultural reference points was embarrassing—I didn't know the musicians, politicians, or historical events that were the touchstones of their lives. What I did know was food and clothes.

I made *ifo* stew worth fighting over, seasoned Nigerian style—if it didn't make the bridge of my nose sweat at the first taste, it wasn't hot enough. I could tie a head wrap better than many native Nigerian girls at school, and several girls remarked that I owned more Nigerian clothes than they did. I began to read up on Nigeria's history, and talked to my mom about what it had been like for her over there. I wanted to fill in the gaps between my experiences as an African and the actual culture, of which I did not possess a deep understanding. Eventually I ran for office in the ASU. I dismissed the tinge of resentment I felt from some of the women as general female animosity until I overheard a group of them talking about me. "She's not really Nigerian," one girl said. "She doesn't even speak any language." "She's just mixed," another added. She said the last word like I was something dirty.

I was mad enough to fight, and sick to my stomach. In that instant I felt totally negated. Africa was the stick I had been beaten with for years. I had suffered for being African, and yet continued to rep Nigeria to the fullest. After all these years, now I wasn't Nigerian enough? Hadn't I earned the right to claim it, by my tears?

It had never occurred to me that none of that would count to culturally immersed, ethnically identified Nigerians. To them, I was an outsider, an impostor, an American with an African name.

I examined my heart, and found I still felt Nigerian. My first concepts of family and my self-worth all came from that source: my grandfather's songs, the gold hoops I had worn since infancy, my aunt peeling mangoes and placing each slice carefully on my tongue. But the soundtrack to my life was indelibly American, full of my grandmother's classic blues albums and then, later, hip-hop. I began to realize that I could not base my identity on what people said I was or wasn't. Being called an African booty-scratcher wasn't what made me African, and a couple of girls questioning my legitimacy couldn't undo my identity.

I still say, if asked, that I am Nigerian. It is my birthplace, my lineage, and it's the answer people are looking for when they wonder about the origin of my name or my physical features. But I am also as American as sweet potato pie. My existence adds to the possibilities of what can be: Nigerian girls can have Southern values and radical politics, and African American women can be personally invested in the global fight against sexism, ethnocentrism, and class prejudice.

In fact, being at the juncture of these two cultures has given me a fuller stake in this war than, I believe, either one alone would have. I am ready to see us advance. Come, let us go. Perhaps that was the plan all along.

# A LESSON IN POSTURE

## Jenesha de Rivera

I'm THIRTY-THREE AND MY SHOULDERS still slouch. When I was a kid, my mother told me I had terrible posture. She saw it as a symbol of weakness; bad posture was unattractive and unladylike. My mother is extremely proud and strong willed. I, on the other hand, tend to be modest and soft-spoken. *"Anak,"* my mother would say pleadingly, "when you walk, please straighten your shoulders. Don't walk like that *mura kag kawatan og manok.*" My mother thought she could correct my posture by telling me I looked like a chicken thief. The lesson in posture never stuck, but the impression of the chicken thief did.

When I was young the image was irrelevant to me. First of all, nobody in Orangeburg, New York, had chickens. And if they did, why would anyone want to steal them? Eventually, I understood it was a Filipino saying that my mother had brought with her from Mindanao, where she was raised. I picture myself as the chicken thief: I'm skinny and hungry. My hair is greasy. I shuffle and drag my flip-flops along a dusty, unpaved road. My head bows down, avoiding any eye contact. My shoulders curve inward and my brown, ashy arms clutch a feisty feathered bird to my chest.

My mother was born in a Philippine province called Lanao del Norte, located on the northern tip of Mindanao, the country's second-largest island. Although the country is predominantly Catholic, the southern islands including Mindanao have a large Muslim population. The Muslims in Mindanao are commonly referred to as Moro or Maranao, the name of an ethnic group in Lanao. Before my mother was born, Lanao was a province of the Moro district—a territory that protected the Muslims from the Catholic conquistadors. Western colonization later divided this territory into north and south, segregating populations: Catholic from Muslim—or, as the early Spanish colonizers saw it, civilized from savage. This colonial mentality wove itself into the culture. It informed my mother's perceptions of herself, the world, and me.

My mom's views of Maranao people are unflattering. She sees them as *pangit*, the opposite of the Filipina mestiza beauty. Typically, in the Philippines, beauty is equated with how *tangos*, or pointy, your nose is. A narrow, petite nose is viewed as an asset, whereas a wide nose is seen as something to hide. "*Hoy*, don't smile so big, your nose is getting wider!" my mother often warned. Beauty in the Philippines is also associated with light skin. If there had been a Keep-Your-Daughter-Out-of-the-Sun club, my mother would have been president. A few years ago, during a trip to the Philippines, I noticed that all the popular *artistas* whose faces graced tabloid covers had smooth, creamy skin. I asked my mom if there had ever been an aesthetic of dark-skinned beauty. "Sweetheart," she answered, "when you are dark, you are not pretty here." As we walked through the drugstore aisles, I noticed skin-lightening creams and *singit* whiteners, a cream that is marketed to women as a remedy for the dark folds and wrinkles of the skin under the armpits, on the elbows, and near the groin. The labels on the boxes boasted No Dark Spot in Seven Days! This marketing myth scorned the sight of dark skin. Men like my uncles perpetuated this belief by stating their reasons for wanting to date white women: "Their *singit* is *malinis*, not dark and dirty looking like the crease between a Filipina's thighs."

Though my mother isn't exactly cream colored, her skin isn't as brown as mine. When I was eight, I went to the Philippines for the second time. After a few short days under the sun, my skin turned from the color of light coffee to the color of a burnt coffee bean.

"*Hoy*, you look like a Moro!" my mother said. "Be careful, they might think you're one of theirs and steal you!" My relatives laughed and made it an ongoing joke during my stay. To them it was funny to see the American kid from the States become as dark as the natives. "*Daghan Maranao didto!*" my mother said, an insinuation that the population of Muslims multiplied the way roaches did in our apartment.

It was during this trip that I acquired an understanding of Cebuano, the dialect of my mother's province. At first, the way my mother and her siblings used the word Maranao made me think they were referring to animals. It rhymed with the word for water buffalo, *carabao*, and in my mind I learned to make this association. The huge, dark brown oxen were used to pull large carts of rice, coconuts, or mangoes, or even truckloads of people. Their wide, round nostrils were big enough for a farmer to thread thickly braided ropes through. The ropes were then fastened to the overloaded wagons. The bulls were sturdier than horses and, despite their girth, could scale steep, narrow, mountainous terrain effortlessly. However, the customary practice of overloading their wagons caused the animals to strain. I felt sorry for these struggling bulls, their heads pulled backward from the weight.

I also felt pity for the Maranao people. I understand now how language can create separation. Categorizing people divides us, and certain associations establish a sense of otherness. I don't think any of the adults understood the consequences of their language, or how it would translate in my eight-year-old mind. I know now that Maranao people represented something shameful to my family. Like an overloaded wagon, this shame dragged down my family's shoulders. In an attempt to lighten the load they chose to act as if Maranao people had nothing to do with their history. As if being Maranao had nothing to do with being Filipino. As a child I learned the tools of language pretty quickly. Not only did I find commonality between a *carabao* and a Maranao, but I was taught enough to believe that the very image I felt sorry for had nothing to do with me.

Of my mother's five siblings, only one sister had skin as dark as mine. "*Baka* your Tita Luz is really a daughter of the Moros," my mom would joke. "Growing up we always wondered if she might have been adopted." Tita Luz was the black sheep in the family. I remember the deep rattle of her husky smoker's voice and how I enjoyed bouncing in the passenger seat of her Jeep Wrangler. She was also a heavy drinker, cursed unabashedly, and was later labeled a bad mother when she divorced her husband. I identified with her. I was a stubborn tomboy who preferred to collect Matchbox cars rather than Barbie dolls. I liked to run around topless and vehemently refused to wear the custom-made dresses my grandmother gave me for Christmas. When the family laughed about the increasing darkness of my skin, it was Tita Luz who came to my defense. "Come on, Jinks, let's go join the Moros. Maybe they'll treat us better than these *estúpidos*."

I was sure she meant it. My grandmother's enormous house in Mindanao stood out among the huts and fields surrounding it. Nearby was a corner store that looked more like the huts I saw on *Gilligan's Island* than any stores I knew. Inside there was an old woman who sold candy, chocolate bars, and coconut juice. Although it was only a few yards from my *lola's* house, I was never allowed to walk there on my own. An aunt or one of my *lola's* maids had to accompany me.

"There's one," Tita Luz whispered as we walked down the dirt path to the corner store. She pointed with her chin toward a woman wrapped in a rich red garment that covered most of her body and draped over her head. She was holding an infant. "Those are their houses." Tita Luz was referring to their tiny *nipa* huts, rickety straw squares that looked more like doghouses than places families could call home. "We call them squatters because they aren't allowed to live here. But they fight with the government and threaten to kill us, so we just leave them alone.

"And there's another one," Tita Luz said, gesturing toward a young girl. I watched her as she walked toward us. Her dress was tattered; the dark color of her skin contrasted with the light brown dirt powdering her knees. In that moment I understood what it meant to be American. If she'd had clothes like me, a house with running water, and a real bathtub, she could have looked just like me. The little girl stared at me as she passed. I squeezed my *tita's* hand tighter and thought: *And I could look like her.* "You see why the others make jokes?" my *tita* said. "You're almost as dark as they are. Never mind, at least you're pretty!" She laughed, grabbed my hand, and sped up. "We better hurry before we make them mad."

Fights often broke out between the Moros and the government officials. There were rumors that people were held hostage until the Moros' demands were met.

"Why are they mad?" I asked my mother.

"Because they don't have any more land. *Kawawa naman* they are," she said, offering a tiny bit of sympathy. "*Pero*, they act like savages. How can there be any peace if they behave like that?"

My mother's sense of pity for the Moros was lined with the belief that we were better—and somehow more legitimate. By learning to hate their struggle instead of understanding it, we all lost the opportunity to honor the legacy of one of the most valiant struggles of the Philippines itself. The Moros' armed struggle for land was an effort to resist assimilation to Western colonization. Filipino Muslims are portrayed in the American media as indignant savages. To this day, the Muslims continue to feel alienated from the Philippine government, which is marked by Christian customs and rituals. Their representation in the media as gun-toting terrorists who take people hostage is still very much alive.


Back in New York, my mother's feelings about the Moros shaped her worldview. She tested me with rhetorical questions. "When you grow up, what kind of man do you think you'll marry?" I couldn't answer. It was the furthest thing from my mind. I looked at her and shrugged my shoulders. "If he is Filipino, it's okay," she continued. "When I'm old, I can live with you and he won't mind. If he is white, it's okay, too, but maybe he won't let me stay. Just remember, never marry a black man, your kids will grow up to look like Moros."

My mother was especially proud of Gloria Diaz, the first Filipina to win the Miss Universe pageant, in 1969. I watched many beauty pageants on television with my mother, and she always talked about Gloria's accomplishments. "She was a true mestiza beauty." My mother dreamed of the possibility that I might one day rise to the challenge. She clung to this fantasy the same way some white families dreamed of their sons becoming president. My mother was determined to squeeze me into the image of the darling daughter she'd always wished for. However, my growing collection of unworn dresses was evidence of her failed attempts and of my unyielding tenacity. After the inevitable struggle to coax me into one, she would make me saunter into the living room while she sang the Miss America anthem. "There she is, Miss America," my mother sang, while I hunched and slouched in mock procession. I knew that you could only be Miss Universe after you won the Miss America crown and that you could only be Miss America after winning a local pageant that wasn't televised in New York. "If not Miss Universe, Miss America is okay, too," my mother would say reassuringly. Despite the fact that I was lactose intolerant, my mother insisted that I drink milk to increase my height. "That's why all the Americans (in this case she meant white people) are tall and have such nice skin," she said. "You can't win Miss America if you are *putót* and have *tigidig*."

I was nine when my mother bought me the Snow White magic mirror. A white woman's face crowned with Crayola-yellow hair would light
up and say: "You are the prettiest of them all." I enjoyed the toy more for
its magic than for its compliments. The toy meant a lot to my mother, so
I tried to like it. I spent hours in front of the mirror. "You are the prettiest of them all," the mirror said. I stared at my face superimposed over the
blond fairy godmother's. Her face was oval and the arches of her cheeks
were high, angular cliffs; her nose was steep and narrow. In contrast, my
face was round and flat. The flesh on my nose was thick and hard. The
arch of my nose barely rose above the cushioning of my cheeks. My eyes
were dark and didn't glitter like hers. I'd stare at myself for long periods
of time. Each time, my image became lost behind the animated glow of
the fairy godmother's face. My mother said, "Practice pinching your nose
every day so when you grow up it won't be so wide." I contorted my face,
widening my eyes while I pinched and raised my nose. "Will I be prettier
this way?" I asked my reflection.

In fourth grade, Kenia Urena was assigned to the desk next to mine.
I remember being surprised by the fact that she was black but spoke
Spanish fluently. "My *mami* is from the Dominican Republic," she told
me. Unlike me, Kenia talked a lot. Her mother worked in the same
hospital as my mother. This Upper East Side hospital subsidized the
apartment building my family lived in. Kenia and I attended a Catholic elementary school a block away from my apartment. The students in
my class were predominantly children of Latino and black immigrants
who lived in the boroughs of Queens, Brooklyn, and the Bronx. Many
of these immigrants worked as orderlies or as nurses at the surrounding
hospitals. In fact, there were very few people of color living in the Upper East Side. They were either nannies coming to care for white children, people who worked at the hospital, or students going to school.

By the time I was eight, my mother let me walk home alone. Kenia
and her mother lived uptown—"In the hundreds and forties," she told
me. One day I invited Kenia over. When we walked in, my mother looked
surprised to see me with someone else. I never brought friends home.

Kenia was slightly taller than me. She had big round eyes that smiled when her mouth did. Her skin was about three shades darker than mine, and her hair was straightened into an unnatural shape that curled and waved. My mother paused for a moment to assess my new friend. Then Kenia and I sat in the living room while my mother rushed around the apartment. She finished preparing dinner—a pot of chicken adobo for my father and me to eat while she was at work—and got ready for her 4:30 shift. I brought out the magic mirror. When I pushed the button and the fairy godmother appeared, Kenia's eyes lit up with delight.

"This is so cool!" she said. "Did your *mami* buy this for you?"

"Yeah, but I don't really like it."

"Why not?" she asked. "Was it expensive?"

"I don't know," I shrugged. "If you really like it you can have it."

"Really?" she asked, pushing the button again.

"You are the prettiest of them all," the mirror said.

Kenia thanked me and pulled the mirror closer to her so she could see her reflection. My mother and I stood at the door when Kenia's mom picked her up. Kenia turned toward me, embraced the mirror with both of her arms, and smiled broadly as she said goodbye. When they were gone, my mother looked at me sternly.

"Why did she take your toy?"

"I gave it to her."

"Are you sure?" my mother asked. "You know black people want to take your things. If you give them something, they will think they can take everything. Don't ever bring her back here."

My mother's anger took me by surprise. It confused me. By giving away my toy it seemed as if I had done something bad. I wondered if I had made a mistake by choosing Kenia to be my friend. The next day at school I told Kenia what my mother had said.

"You're not allowed to come over anymore."

"Why not?" she asked.

"Because you're black." My words unleashed themselves like double-edged daggers piercing both of us.

My cheeks burned as though someone had slapped them as we stood there silently staring at each other. The chatter of students' voices filled the hush between us, and in that moment I felt completely alone. As the news about my mom made its way around the class, my isolation grew. My classmates' rejection was crushing. Offering the magic mirror to Kenia was an act of generosity. What did Kenia see in that mirror? What did I see when I looked at Kenia? I saw myself. In the face of my mother's rejection I felt powerless. I hated that I was unable to change the curse that plagued me, that labeled me dark, unlovable, and unworthy of friendship. In this state of powerlessness, I targeted my anger at Kenia, the girl who was just like me. Although she was Dominican and I was Filipina, I understood that the darker you were the less you were loved.

Ultimately, the loss of my mother's acceptance was the most painful experience of all. I came to believe that her love was based on a conditional standard that I could never measure up to. As a child and an adolescent, I felt I had to choose between earning the acceptance of other people and earning the love of my mother. I discovered that when I chose one or the other, there was still an emotional vacancy inside of me. My mother's beliefs about beauty prevented me from seeing anything beautiful in myself. The way I looked at the world and at other people was tainted. Through it I experienced the loss of friendship and generosity.

I know now that my mother's lessons in posture and beauty were expressions of an underlying anger and self-hate, of all the images she may have tried to live up to but failed. My mother didn't choose or create the society she lived in. She inherited it. As a nine-year-old, my inheritance of unrealistic and self-diminishing standards suffocated me. I knew my mother's beauty queen dreams were unrealistic. It was as if the fantasy had become a perpetrator ridiculing and taunting me for my inability to measure up to its false standards. Within me, it planted a growing seed of self-hate and frustration. My lack of self-acceptance left me emotionally vulnerable and unsafe, and so in anger and fear I protected myself from anything or anybody that threatened to take what sense of safety I had left.

In high school I also struggled with my sexuality as well as my in-securities about my looks. The self-loathing I felt about my appearance added to the intense shame I felt as a closeted lesbian. Fortunately, I found a network of supportive friends in college who helped me to accept my sexuality and butch gender expression. At the age of twenty-one, I came out to my mother. She didn't have an easy time accepting me as a lesbian. It only exacerbated and confirmed her long-standing argument regarding my lack of femininity. "Tomboy," the term for lesbian in the Philippines, evoked many unfavorable associations in my mother. Unfortunately, her limited knowledge led her to associate my identity with my appearance. "Back home," she'd say, "only women who are too ugly to find a man become tomboy. How come you want to be a tomboy, *anak*? You're *guapa naman*. After all, you're pretty." I couldn't believe my ears. Although it was a conditional, albeit homophobic statement about my beauty, it was the first time I *heard* her say it. They say that instinctually every mother believes her child is beautiful. In my heart I know this is true, but at the time I struggled to believe it. My mother didn't write the rules she lived with. At the time neither of us knew how to change them. Fortunately, on this day we began to learn to break them.

Coming out in college was not the final destination in my journey toward self-acceptance. It was my first step. Telling my mother came next. Although this shattered my mother's idealistic expectations, it opened an enormous door for us. When I was twenty-one I wrote a letter to my mother. In part, it read:

> I love you and no matter how old I am or how far away
> I go I will always need you. That is why I told you. I am
> telling you I am a lesbian so that you can know me and
> see me for who I am. I want you to love me for that. I
> want to know that telling you was not a mistake. That
> it will not ruin our relationship forever because if any-
> thing I had only hoped it would bring us closer.

My mother assumed that, as a lesbian, I would have a life filled with loneliness and isolation. She never intended to hurt me with her words. She only wanted to protect me. I finally understood. The moment before I came out, I thought about my safety, too: I could take what I perceived as the less risky path and acquiesce to the conventional straight majority, or I could accept who I was, face adversity, and create my own destiny. In Mindanao, the Moros were faced with similar options. Although a great number were massacred for choosing the latter, many more have kept the indigenous heritage alive because of their choice. I began to understand that my mother's desire to protect me influenced her notions about beauty, femininity, and skin color. Although her lessons were painful, I know now that they were also acts of love.

I don't profess that it was easier to accept my sexuality than it was to accept my brown skin. Although society finds many ways to fragment my identity, in my experience the parts are never separate. My beauty is not dependent on my height, the color of my skin, or whom I choose to be intimate with.

Occasionally I'm reminded of the chicken thief. As my mother's daughter, I realize there is an imaginary line that separates this image and me. I carry this image through the streets that I walk, in my shoulders that still slouch, and in my skin that responds to the sun. When I was younger, I learned to feel shame instead of pride and to separate myself from my culture instead of connecting with it. I mourn these losses. However, it is through my lesson in posture that I actively seek to regain it all.

# UNDER THE *MANDAP*

## Sona Pai

ON MY WEDDING DAY, in my hometown of St. Joseph, Missouri, I hold a coconut instead of a bouquet as I walk down a petal-speckled aisle with slow, deliberate steps. As the *pandit* who is performing the ceremony recites eight verses of Sanskrit blessings, cameras flash in a mosaic of light around me. Guests—Indian and non-Indian alike—repeat a Sanskrit phrase at the end of each verse. In shaky unison, they sing their blessings to me in an ancient tongue, punctuating the *pandit's* melodic verses. My parents thought I'd have to fast before the ceremony, as is often required before such solemn Hindu rituals. But months before, the *pandit* had assured me that it was not necessary to fast, so two hours before the wedding, I stood alone in my parents' kitchen, eating a bowl of Cheerios over the sink. Still, I feel faint and feverish as I walk down the aisle, as though beads of sweat are puddling under my red *ghagra choli*, all soft and swish and heavy with shiny crystals sewn into georgette crepe.

Two of my mother's brothers, my *mamas*, escort me to the *mandap*, the four-post structure that creates the sacred space for the ceremony. *Mandaps* aren't easy to come by in St. Joe, so my dad spent months designing a frame out of nine-foot stalks of bamboo. In the days before the wedding, my parents assembled the *mandap* on the stage of the old Christian Science Church, the only place in town that could hold our more than three hundred guests and that would also allow us to light a small fire for the ceremony. My parents decorated the *mandap* with help from my local uncles and aunties—the ones related to me not by blood but by more than twenty years of birthday parties and Indian potlucks and Diwali celebrations and Thanksgivings. They covered the church's ugly old radiators with heavy cloth embroidered with elephants and flowers and embedded with dime-sized mirrors. They draped the posts of the *mandap* with slippery soft tulle that billowed and shimmered ivory. They hung twisted lengths of batik fabric drenched molten red. And behind the *mandap*, they concealed a quote about Jesus with a creamy white tapestry embellished with golden thread.

With a *mama* on either side, I inch down the aisle cupping the coconut in my hands, both of which are inked mahogany with swirls of henna. A Hindu priest blessed the coconut at a prayer ceremony two days before the wedding, a *puja* held at my parents' home to bless our family and set the planets in auspicious alignment for my marriage. I'm not sure exactly what the coconut is for or what it means, but I was told to hold it, so I do. Later, I'm told that the coconut is known as God's fruit, a tangible connection to the divine.

At the front of the church, gingerly and very seriously, as though I am some delicate and precious thing, my uncles help me slip off my shoes and then ease me up the steps to the stage, into the sacred space of the *mandap*, and onto my seat opposite Mike. He's already been through the first twenty minutes of the ceremony with the *pandit* and my parents. He sat and watched as my parents followed the *pandit's* instructions in a series of rituals to welcome Lord Ganesh, remover of obstacles and god of good fortune. They slurped small sips of water that the *pandit* spooned into their hands. They recited the many names of the divine. They used red *kumkum* paste and grains of rice to anoint a betel nut, another representation of the divine. They vowed to entrust Mike with my hand in marriage.

As I make my way to the *mandap*, Mike sits hidden from my view behind a sheet of white silk. My mother and father stand holding one corner of the sheet, beaming proud but sad smiles, and Mike's parents hold up the other corner. The *pandit* explains what is about to happen in this ceremony with four thousand years of precedent, and I contemplate the scene in front of me: our parents holding the thin but opaque barrier between us—between this brown girl and this freckly, red-haired white boy, between first-generation Indian American and Scottish German American, several generations removed. The *pandit* explains that, in earlier times, a Hindu wedding would have been arranged by the parents, and the bride and groom would have seen each other for the first time right here, in the middle of their own wedding ceremony. Everyone laughs, because Mike and I have been dating for nine years. I try to picture Mike's face, but all I can see are his wringing hands and jittery knees under the wall of the silk sheet.

Born and raised in America, the child of Indian immigrants, I grew up inside and outside two different cultures. My parents spoke to each other in Gujarati at home and in a lilting, British English everywhere else; I talked back to them like a valley girl-wannabe. I ate drab cafeteria lunches at school and came home for chapatis, spiced vegetables tinted yellow with turmeric, and chicken curry that I could smell before I walked in the front door. Every day, I spent hours on the phone with my friends talking about clothes and boys and music, and every other Sunday I spent a few minutes on the phone with my grandparents in India, saying little more than "Hi. How are you? I'm fine." In high school, I told my friends I couldn't go to parties because I had to baby-sit, when really it was because my parents didn't approve. When I went out, I told my parents it wasn't a date when it really was.

As my wedding ceremony begins, that feeling of living two lives at once crystallizes, and the two halves of my history stand in sharp relief. I feel like the fairy-tale American bride, eager to profess my love for a man who respects me and takes care of me, and who already knows the ugliest things about me and loves me anyway. At the same time, as I sit clothed in bridal red, with henna on my hands, bangles on my wrists, black kohl lining my eyes, silver bells around my ankles, and girlhood in my past, I feel connected to all Indian brides, separated from the mysteries of my future by just a slim veil of white silk.

Four months before the wedding, my mom and I are sitting with my Auntie Janu, my father's younger sister, in a store called Friendship, a multilevel maze in the Mumbai suburb of Santa Cruz. This is my fourth trip to India. The first was at age two, when I sipped from a straw stuck right into a round green coconut heavy with sweet water; the second was at age eleven, when mustard seeds got stuck in my braces and my bangs fell flat in the humid air; the third was at age twenty-four, when I spent a summer becoming more familiar with my family.

Now, for my fourth visit, I am twenty-seven, here to shop for my wedding with a shopping list that includes, among other items: wedding outfits for me, my mom, my dad, my brother, Mike's mom, and Mike's sister; outfits for two bridesmaids, two groomsmen, and four flower girls (none of which are typically part of a Hindu wedding, but are included at my request); wedding bangles, anklets, earrings, necklace, and *tikka*, a gold ornament on a chain that will hook into my hair at the crown and hang in the center of my forehead; a copper vessel in which to build the fire, the centerpiece and divine witness of the ceremony; tapestries and faux-flower garlands for decorating the church and my parents' home; twenty-five whole, raw betel nuts; two ounces each of an assortment of powders (red *kumkum*, pink *gulal*, orange *sindhoor*, white *abil*, and yellow *haldi*); six small stainless steel bowls and spoons; two yards of fine white silk; two small, shallow terra-cotta bowls that will be filled with flowers, rice, and *kumkum* and bound together with cloth (Mike will smash the earthen package with his foot when he enters the church); Indian wedding music to play in the house all week before the wedding; and plastic cones filled with henna paste to decorate my hands and feet.

My mom and I have two weeks to complete our scavenger hunt, and we begin in the air-conditioned room reserved for brides-to-be at Friendship. We sit on a densely stuffed mattress on the floor, in front of a salesman who's eager to please. He insists that we have a snack, and even though we decline, he sends a young man to fetch toasted vegetable-and-chutney sandwiches, hot chai, and cold sodas from a vendor on the street. We're surrounded by walls of flat red boxes, stacked floor to ceiling. My mom and Auntie Janu do the talking in Hindi, which I understand in bits and pieces but do not speak. She's getting married soon, they say, in America. She wants something nice, something elegant and red.

From the stacked boxes, the salesman's assistants pull out half-stitched *ghagra cholis* ready to be customized to my measurements. The garments are lovely and flattering: high-waisted, long, A-line skirts, or *ghagras*, ornate with shiny embroidery, sequins, crystals cut like diamonds, and tiny mirrors; fitted, cap-sleeved cropped tops, or *cholis*, to match; and, to complete each ensemble, a flowing, sparkling length of fabric to pleat and drape like a sari. The men show me outfits made of violet organza and pink crepe. I speak up and say I want to wear red, the traditional color for Hindu brides. The salesman tells me red is old-fashioned and, these days, modern brides wear modern colors. He shows me yellow and green, purple and peach, but I'm not interested. Finally he gives in and produces a range of outfits in red—pale winter-tomato red, burgundy-wine red, and a red so dark it looks brown. His young male assistants model the outfits for me, deftly securing them to their bodies with clips and straps. Another assistant sits beside us folding the outfits I've rejected and placing them neatly back in their red boxes.

There are two other shoppers in the bridal room, both from America, and both accompanied by a flock of opinionated mothers and cousins and aunties and friends of aunties. I eavesdrop on their conversations, wondering where they're from in America and if they're marrying Indian guys. One is holding up a gauzy white *ghagra choli* embroidered in red, gold, and green. Her eyes are wide and dazzled as she admires herself in the mirror, and I can tell she's found what she's looking for. We all could have found our bridal wear in America, in the Indian sections of Los Angeles or Chicago or New York. But they probably would have been more expensive and not as nice, ready-made and not tailored just for us. In India, we know we'll find the perfect outfit, and we can share the excitement with our faraway family members, many of whom might not be able to travel to America for our weddings.

As the poor guy in charge of folding struggles to keep up with my pile of rejects, finally, and with a flourish, the salesman pulls the outfit I'll wear for my wedding out of what seems like the last box in the room. It's a ripe, fruity red, as though it were dyed from the juice of pomegranates or the pressed flesh of wild strawberries. Triangular panels of crystals arranged in shapes that look like diamonds and pineapples fan out from the waist to the hem. The georgette crepe is smooth and cool to the touch; the *choli* blouse is simple and framed with crystals at the neck and sleeves. The final touch is a sleek piece of matching, satiny red fabric weighed down by a border of crystals and a pattern of tiny crystal flowers, like fancy polka dots. My mom and Auntie Janu see my dreamy gaze and wide grin, and they laugh as they share a knowing look. They tell the salesman to hold the *ghagra choli* for us and say we'll be back in a few days if we don't find something better.

The days that follow are a whirlwind of traffic, tea, richly colored fabrics, and much-needed midday naps as, one by one, we cross items off our list. Now we're looking at outfit after outfit at Amarsons, Benzer, Ritu Kumar, Shital, and Kalaniketan, with comfortable chairs and cold bottles of sweet, tart Limca at each store. Now we're trying to keep up with my mother's elderly aunt, shrunken with cancer but quick on her feet as she leads us through a busy bazaar to a shop lined with glass jars of herbs, spices, and colored powders. Now we're in a tiny storefront piled high with stainless steel vessels of all sizes. Now Amma, my father's mother, is helping me try on a gold *tikka*, her wedding gift to me. Now we're haggling with a fabric merchant for a couple of yards of white silk. Now we're watching Kaka, my mother's father, swat a meandering cow with his walking stick as he leads us through another bazaar in search of mirrored tapestries and flower garlands. Now we're buying two small terra-cotta bowls from a crouched, gray-haired woman behind a vegetable market. She blesses me and tells me I must bring her sweets after my marriage. Now Ba, my mother's mother, is examining the gold filigree bangles I've picked out—her gift to me—and telling me they look old-fashioned. Now she's playing me a tape of the songs she'll listen to on my wedding day. They sound joyful, but she tells me the words are sad, about a girl leaving her mother and father to live with her husband and his family.

I fly back to America with my wedding outfit and jewelry in my carry-on bag, along with plastic bags filled with sweet *mithai* and crunchy snack mixtures of fried strands of spiced chickpea batter, matchstick potatoes, groundnuts, and golden raisins. As the dim lights of Mumbai recede below me, I think about how lucky I am to be able to make such a trip, and how I wish my grandparents could make the long journey to my wedding. I think about Ba sitting at home listening to bittersweet ballads, and I wish that I had thought to ask my grandmothers about their own weddings. I wish I knew how they felt as they approached the *mandap*; what they were thinking in those few fleeting moments between their lives as girls and their lives as wives; if they were a little scared to traverse the terrain that lay beyond the white silk.

When I return from India, I start working on our wedding program, eager to learn about the ceremony and to explain it for our American guests. I read about the ceremony's roots in the ancient text of the *Atharvaveda* and reread the wedding scene between Rama and Sita in the *Ramayana*. I muddle through a cultural anthropology text about the roles and rituals of Hindu women. I scour the Internet and look back on the notes I saved from college courses about Indian civilization, religion, and philosophy. I watch a thirty-year-old home movie of my parents' wedding ceremony, grainy and without sound. None of it really helps, but at least I feel like I've done my homework. In the end, I just rewrite the steps from programs my mom has saved from other weddings over the years. I also follow the convenient outline the *pandit* gave me when we met a few months before.

In my first meeting with him, and in subsequent conversations with my parents and other relatives, I express concern and discomfort with one part of the ceremony. Called *Kanya Daan*, it is the step in which the bride's parents formally offer their daughter to the bridegroom. In my research, I find explanations of this step that use words like "relinquish," "give away," and "hand over." I object to this notion not because of my feminist sensibilities, but because I don't believe that my wedding will alter my relationship with my family. My elders smile as they assure me that the words mean only what I want them to mean and that, in any case, there is no way to change the traditional ceremony. This is not like the Western ceremonies I've seen, open for editing, with quick vows, tossed bouquets, and a kiss to seal the deal. The Hindu ceremony is about a girl becoming a woman, about growing out of one phase of life and into another.

Growing up, I had always thought of my life between two cultures as a role without a script. Now, at twenty-seven, it becomes clear to me that this was not really the case. As my hyphenated identity took shape over the years, clues were everywhere. Pop culture and peer pressure taught me what was cool and American; parental expectations and family traditions taught me what was proper and Indian. At school with my friends and at home with my family, I always did what I thought I was supposed to do, and I had plenty of guides to provide direction. Now, as I plan all the details of my wedding ceremony, I begin to think of what will come after it. No one and nothing will be there to show me how to be an Indian American wife to an American man or how to be a mother to our children—the second generation—who will be half as Indian as I am.

After growing up wondering if I could ever be American enough to fit in with my friends, now I wonder if I can ever be Indian enough to give my children the culture of their ancestors. I can cook a full Indian meal, but I need all day to do it. I can speak a little Gujarati and even less Hindi, but barely enough to complete a full sentence. I can wear a sari, but only if someone else puts it on for me. I start to wonder if I'm ready for this leap from daughter and sister to wife and mother. I should have tried to speak Gujarati when I was young, I think, and I should have learned more from my mother, aunties, and grandmothers. I start to feel hopelessly unprepared, unsure how to be the person I will become when it's over. Then I think about the Indian philosophy course I took in college and a passage I had written in bold letters and circled with stars in my notebook. It's from the *Ashtavakra Gita*, an ancient Sanskrit text that presents the teachings of the Advaita Vedanta, the philosophy that the individual and the divine and everything else in the universe are one and the same: "If you think you are free, you are free / If you think you are bound, you are bound." The ceremony will mean what I want it to mean, and the life after it will be mine to design.

Before the *pandit* removes the silk veil between us, held in place by our smiling yet somber parents, he says it's his responsibility to ask Mike a question: "Mike, do you want to run? Are you sure you're okay with this?" The audience cracks up. The *pandit* peppers the ceremony with jokes like this, to lighten the mood and keep the audience awake through the long event. From behind the veil, I hear Mike say he's ready in a shaky voice. We're each given a heavy garland of red and white carnations in full bloom. Then, as the *pandit* recites more Sanskrit verses, he takes the veil from our parents' hands—the barrier of family and culture and history that stands between us—and drapes it around my neck for the duration of the ceremony. I see Mike for the first time all day. He is clean-shaven and wearing an ivory *sherwani* suit, with a knee-length jacket embroidered in red and gold at the collar and down the center. A long maroon batik scarf hangs around his neck.

In the hour and a half to come, we'll participate in a series of ancient rituals, all of us watching the *pandit* closely for directions. My parents will formally entrust Mike with my hand in marriage. A corner of my garment will be tied to Mike's scarf, symbolizing our new unity. Mike will invoke the presence of Lord Ganesh and the divine fire, Agni, as he adds clarified butter to fuel the flame. My twenty-two-year-old brother, Neil, will enter the *mandap* for his part in the *Mangal Fera*, a ritual in which Mike and I walk around the fire four times to represent the ultimate goals in the Hindu life: righteousness, prosperity, love, and spiritual liberation. Neil will pour grains of rice, a symbol of his love and support, into my hands before each round, and I will then offer the rice to the fire. The *pandit* will tell the guests that this symbolizes the fact that my brother is giving me up to my husband, a statement that makes me uncomfortable in its finality because I didn't know it was coming, and I don't believe it's true. Mike will clasp a *mangal sutra*, a necklace of black and gold beads, around my neck, and sprinkle bright orange *sindhoor* along the part in my hair. These are the quintessential symbols of a married Indian woman. As Mike and I dutifully do as the *pandit* tells us in each of these and other rituals, the rest of the ceremony will fly by. But in that first moment after the white veil is dropped, it feels for a second as though we are on our own.

I think about how much we've grown up together and how we've been dating all of my adult life. I think about how my family has welcomed him so warmly, and how fortunate I am that this marriage was not arranged, but rather happily accepted, by my parents. I think about how he will be the father of my children. I think about what a good sport he's being, and how he knows even less about this ceremony than I do. I think about how he has never once made me feel different or foreign for being Indian in our whitewashed Midwestern surroundings. In a life of searching for cues for how to be Indian or American, how to combine this with that, I find myself in a moment of rare clarity. I reach across the sacred space between us, and with a garland of flowers, I choose Mike and the life we will forge together. I place the garland around his neck, and, in the only unscripted moment of the ceremony, I hold his face in my hands for a quick second, and I know that I'm ready for whatever comes next.

# FOOLING MEXICANS

## María Elena Fernández

SINCE MY FIRST YEAR OF COLLEGE, MY ONLY desire had been to see, touch, and climb the shrines to Mexico's—and my—grand Indian past. My freshman year, I gazed upon them for the first time on a faraway screen in a cavernous Yale University lecture hall, as snow fell steadily outside. Finally, one year after graduation and after five years of dreaming about it, my friend Elva and I prepared for our ancestral journey. Taking buses, we planned to depart from Mexico City and head toward the Pacific coast, follow the Isthmus of Tehuantepec to Yucatán, and culminate our quest on the Caribbean coast. Back home in Los

Angeles, as I packed my bags, I relived moments in the lecture hall when I'd first memorized silhouettes and facades: the precise and intricate patterns on Monte Albán's tall walls, Palenque's breathtaking lattice towers, Uxmal's mysterious geometric doorways, the bold feathered serpents punctuating Chichén Itzá's structures, and Tulum, the tranquil remains of a seaside castle. And once again, with each click of the slide carousel, I fell more and more in love.

I was born and raised in Los Angeles, the daughter of Mexico City immigrants, and Mexican culture was the electrical current that animated our household. Parental affection and scolding, children's pleadings and complaints all took place in Spanish. *"Sana sana colita de rana." "¿¡Todavía no estás lista?!" "¿Puedo jugar otro ratito, por favor?" "¡Mamí! ¡El me pegó primero!"* English was reserved only for intersibling exchanges. The postman delivered our native language in envelopes bordered with green and red, and each of us would take turns deciphering Abuelita's or Tia Chela's handwriting. It blared from the TV set in Jacobo Zabludovsky's unmistakable authoritative newsman's voice or Chespirito's wailing cries as the whiny child character El Chavo del Ocho. And every Saturday morning, Los Panchos, Los Diamantes, and Virginia Lopez crooned their sad boleros from the living room turntable until my mother finished her day's chores. Yes, we ate pancakes and French toast, and sometimes cheeseburgers with Campbell's cream of mushroom soup, but the typical nourishment placed on the dining room table was huevos rancheros, *albóndigas, pollo en mole, lengua en salsa de tomate,* and always *frijolitos* on the side. And there were the biannual trips to Mexico City—el D.F. (*pronounced el de efe*)—ever since I can remember.

Held and swaddled as I was by the culture of my origin, surrounded by others in my Catholic grammar school just like me—children of Latin American and Filipino immigrants fluent in both their languages and cultures—there were also incidents that were like thunder's eternal moment of deafening darkness passing through my body. I tried to dismiss these as though I were waving away a passing fly, but instead they seeded a profound uneasiness in me and engraved themselves in that place where I kept all the memories that I still didn't have language for.

In the first grade, my teacher tore off half of my first name, and for eight years I was called Maria F. because in a class packed with forty students there were two other Marias: Maria S. and Maria J.—until I was old enough, and strong enough, to reclaim my full name in high school. There was the stark absence on the American TV shows and news broadcasts of anyone who looked like me, except the occasional gang member or maid, or maybe a report on illegal border crossers. My first day of high school at a girls' Catholic prep school was also my first day immersed in white middle-class culture. Their cars, their clothes, their neighborhoods instantly informed me that I had less, that I was less. And I will never forget the condescending and chilling, "Oh, I see," from a woman on staff where I was doing volunteer work when I told her I was going to Yale in the fall. Her tone clearly implied that she did not believe I had earned my way.

So when I got to college, joyously aflutter, I learned that I was part of a people with a long history in this country of resisting dehumanization: Garment workers, zoot-suiters, farm workers, and students, like me, battled against being seen as less, being treated as less. I was part of this noble tradition. Ambivalence, confusion, and shame lifted. I learned that our roots bore deep into ancient indigenous cultures complete with their own myths and pantheon of gods and goddesses with formidable and mystical names like Quetzalcoatl, Coatlicue, and Tlaloc. I danced like a butterfly, I was Chicana now. And since those slides first flashed before me during my freshman year, there was no greater yearning in me than to make a pilgrimage to the majestic ruins my ancestors had left as my proud patrimony.

It would be my first time in Mexico without my parents and siblings. The trips to el D.F. that had peppered my Los Angeles childhood were two-week whirlwinds of boisterous gatherings overflowing with aunts and uncles, a multitude of cousins to play with, and tables full of the family's special recipes. I reveled in the sea of loving relatives, extended family

I only had for those fourteen days every two years, since no one had followed our migration to Los Angeles. Yet all the while, my stomach knotted and churned, in part because some of the food was unfamiliar like *chicharron en chile*—and unlike my mom's, the *consomé* was spicy, and the milk, cheese, and butter all tasted funny—but mostly because no matter how much I concentrated, my Spanish wobbled, halted, and tripped each time I spoke. Never was I able to say just what I meant; rarely did I understand their jokes. Yet frequently my cousins found me amusing. Each time I was surprised and embarrassed when laughter erupted around me for reasons I didn't know.

I quickly found out that the simple, everyday conversations of my Los Angeles household were not enough. *"Pásame la sal, por favor." "Ya acabé la tarea, Mami."* "Pass me the salt" and "I finished my homework" were easy. And I could always insert a word in English if I couldn't think of it in Spanish. The shower of compliments from my mom's L.A. friends for speaking the language of the homeland, and so politely, had no meaning in Mexico. Not only did I sometimes miss entire conversations among my cousins because I'd never heard of the Mexican superhero they were talking about, but the basics fouled me up every time. No matter how much I practiced *"rr con rr cigarro, rr con rr barril . . ."* I still couldn't roll my *rr*s right, but at least I could brace myself when I had to utter one. What repeatedly caught me unawares was using the masculine or feminine article before a noun. It seemed easy enough: *el* when it ends in "o" and *la* when it ends in "a." *La casa, el teléfono.* But what if it didn't end in either? And I always forgot about the exceptions. So frequently I said things all wrong. *"No encuentro la azucar." "La agua está bien fría."* One of my aunts would touch my hand and gently correct me, *"Se dice 'el agua,' corazonito."* But when I was with my cousins, they just started laughing, and one would snap, *"¡Así no se dice!"* ("That's not how you say it!")

I wasn't used to getting things wrong. At home I was the smartest girl in the class; only Tony Tse was smarter than me, and Glenn Padama and I competed neck and neck. In fact, I was an orator of sorts, called on to do the readings for school masses ever since I was in the second grade. I was never ridiculed. But in Mexico, among the cousins I adored, I was frequently seen as dumb and foolish.

So when I traveled to Mexico on my own for the first time at age twenty-three, I was determined not only to embark on the sacred quest of my newfound motherland, sink my eyes and bare feet into her stunning, luscious landscapes from Oaxaca to Quintana Roo, and let the radiance of each of my ancestors' monuments fill me up; my mission was for Mexico to claim me. I was reclaiming Mexico, but I knew she didn't recognize me, didn't include me. Because, like the States, Mexico called me other, outsider, *pocha*—that seething indictment reserved for the descendants of *Mexicanos* for losing their language and culture. It was never to my face, but I could feel Mexico's disapproving gaze scorch my skin each time I turned around. And then there were the verbal disclaimers. Whenever my cousins introduced me, they called me "*la prima norteamericana,*" the North American cousin. In Mexico City, I wanted to stop each person walking by me on the sidewalk and command his gaze. "Look at me. Don't you recognize me? Can't you see I'm part of you? It's just that I live over there, that's all."

But I knew that Mexico didn't accept me as I was. A Chicana with stammering fluency, no longer a child, and still tripping over words, still a detectable gringo accent, proving all their stereotypes: "*Se olvidan de la cultura. Son unos pochos. Desprecian al Mexicano. Se creen mucho.*" ("They forget the culture. They're a bunch of *pochos.* They look down on Mexicans. They think they're all that.") I didn't want them to think that about me. I wasn't ashamed of being Chicana, I just didn't want to be *that* kind of Chicana in their eyes. I wanted to be such a *good* Chicana, to recapture my Mexican roots so thoroughly that even the Mexicans would think I was one of them. I wanted their approval.

I had a plan. Not only would I shed my gringo accent in Spanish and amass an arsenal of vocabulary to stop the sputtering search for ordinary words, but I would learn to drop slang and popular references. By the time the summer was over, I wanted to be spewing Spanish with

Mexico City cadences like a *chilanga*. To prove myself further, I was determined to function in Mexico City as well as any Mexican. I would learn to mount the metro system of my parents' city like a native. And on my return from my odyssey with Elva, I'd have photos and stories in hand to prove my knowledge and love of the country's most lavish lands. By the end of the summer, Mexico would say to me, *"Tu nos perteneces."* ("You are one of us.")

Ever the overachiever, I excelled. First, I listened fiercely when my aunt bought fruit at the *mercado*, when my cousin asked for school supplies at the *papelería*, when they ordered at a restaurant. As I ventured out on my own to the *tianguis* down the street I practiced: *"¿Cuánto cuesta? ¿Qué vale?"* all the way, so that these phrases would slide out of my mouth casually and unconsciously, as they did for my relatives. My most fierce listening was reserved for one-on-one conversations. The person meeting my gaze never imagined that my attentiveness went far beyond politeness, that I was searing a hole right through her, studying her every syllable, memorizing the intonation of each sentence, filing away words I was missing, taking note of common colloquialisms.

Then I began to mimic. I expunged all anglicisms from my speech. I started with the most obvious gringo traces, purging the ubiquitous "okay" and instead replacing it with *"orale"* or *"bueno."* This was my first act and the most important cleansing of my speech, because I used the term rampantly and unconsciously, both in English and in Spanish. I was ready to forge forward. I began to string together sentences with *chilango* rhythm and speed—no more halting, no more tripping over words. The trick is to allow the tongue to slither swiftly along the roof of the mouth, to slide through the syllables, not mark each one, and avoid getting stuck like a rubber sole on a wooden dance floor. When searching for words—because, after all, even Mexicans search for words in Spanish—the spaces in between also matter. "Um" is a dead-giveaway gringo sound; I learned to use only "mmm" or "eh," the Mexican sounds for filling up silence, as my eyes wandered in search of my next phrase.

The slang that punctuates Mexican Spanish, like *"Qué padre"* and *"a todo dar,*" was the easiest part to incorporate. But to sound like I was really from there, the important words to say were the made-up ones Mexicans use for everyday things. For example, *la combi* is any minivan, but especially the passenger-packed white VW vans that run routes all over the city. I'd use *el bocho* to talk about the VW bugs so prevalent on Mexico City streets. To be on the safe side, I'd avoid words in Spanish that were also used in English. While it's fine to ask for *el menú* in Spanish, I always preferred to ask for *la carta,* to prevent any suspicion. And definitely no anglicisms like *troca* and *parquear* for me. But I knew I shouldn't purge all anglicisms from my vocabulary; I just had to use the right anglicisms. For example, sweats are called *pans* (although I still don't know if that means just the sweat pants or the whole sweat suit). I could really fool them when I started using shorthand. For example, if I was in a conversation with my cousin and she said she wasn't dating some guy anymore, without missing a beat, I would ask, "*¿Por?*" instead of the full version ("*¿Por qué?*"); without missing a beat, she'd answer me. That's when I started to feel powerful. That's when I knew I had them.

And I basked in the accomplishment of my mission when I learned to fearlessly navigate the city's underground labyrinth, to go from my aunt's house to a bookstore or museum and to my uncle's, then back again (La Raza to Hidalgo to Portales, a *pesero* to Zapata and back to La Raza). Unwittingly, I even outdid my cousins: after completing my pilgrimage, I had been to parts of Mexico that they had never even seen.

I've returned to Mexico City each year since that first trip. So for more than ten years I've been fooling Mexicans: the woman I buy the paper from on the corner, the taxi driver who doesn't know how to get to my aunt's house on Clave from the *circuito,* the checkout girl at Aurrera, Mexico's version of Kmart. I fool them because now, within two days of arriving, my Spanish slithers and dances off my tongue again. When I get off the metro at La Raza, I know that if I'm on the Indios Verdes side I need to go underneath to the Universidad side so that I can get the right exit to my aunt's. I don't even have to look at the map on the wall, ask one of the guards, hold my breath, and hope I'm right. Recently, when I went to Oaxaca with a Chicana girlfriend, my cousin told her to let me do the talking when bartering: "*No se le nota el acento.*" ("Her accent doesn't show.")

But I don't fool all of them. I probably don't even fool most of them. I learned that indelible lesson about my zealous quest for Mexicanness on my first trip to Oaxaca, the first destination on my Mexican odyssey with Elva.

On one of our evenings there, we went to a *peña* to listen to live music. I draped the *rebozo* I had bought that day around my shoulders: woven cotton and fuchsia, "*rosa mexicano.*" *Now I'll really look like them*, I thought, and imagined myself being admired in the middle of the plaza as a native beauty in my jeans, *rebozo*, and sandals.

There were no available tables, and the waiter asked if we would mind sharing with a young man sitting alone. Elva and I had been telling people that we were teachers living in Mexico City to make us less vulnerable to male predators and potential thieves. We tried to speak to each other in Spanish in public places. It fit my mission perfectly. When we gave him our alibi, he asked us where we taught.

"The southern part of the city."

"Oh really, what school? I live in *el estado de México*, just south of the city." We were stumped and tried to offer an answer with innocuous specificity. Mercifully, he let us off the hook.

"We got caught, didn't we?" I said to Elva as we debriefed our evening.

"We're always gonna get caught. We're not like them. We talk different, we think different, we even walk different. Look at us. How many Mexican women would roam around the country by themselves? They just don't do that." Elva already knew these things; she had lived in Mexico City for a year.

I re-imagined myself in Oaxaca's plaza. The gazes of admiration by the locals turned to whisperings of "*Esa es turista.*" ("That one's a tourist.")

Now when I'm riding the metro, I notice that occasionally I get one of those stares, usually from the eighteen-year-old with deep-hued Indian skin in the super-tight jeans, his hair a little long, leaning against the doors, surveying everyone, his eyes far too savvy for his years. There's something peculiar about her, his look says. "Too middle-class," he thinks. "Too white, too tall. Too MTV. Probably from the suburbs. What's she doing here?" Finally he concludes, *"Quien sabe, como que tiene pinta de estudiante extranjera."* ("Who knows, maybe that's a foreign-student look she's got.")

"Too first-world, actually," I want to respond, and wonder if he ever thinks, *"Esa tiene pinta de Chicana."* ("It's a Chicana look she's got.")

*Pero tampoco soy turista.* But I'm no tourist. Mexico City is familiar territory—after Los Angeles, the city I know the best. Less so perhaps than to L.A., I belong to el D.F. I see myself as one of Mexico's own, a daughter of the country my parents call their homeland. Perhaps I'm more like a granddaughter. But I am not Mexican. Elva will always be right. We talk different, we think different, we even walk different. And no *rebozo* will change that.

# Rising and Falling

## Anne Liu Kellor

When I get the "What are you?" question, I almost always answer, "I'm half Chinese." This is the half that I know people are interested in, the half that distinguishes me from the other faces around me. If my listeners seem as if they are waiting for the second half of the equation, I will go on to explain, "and half Caucasian," or "and half Euro-American, a mix of stuff, Austrian, Bohemian, French Canadian, etc., you know?" Yes, they'll nod understandingly, because usually they are the same: a mix of ethnicities, far enough removed from their roots that the specifics no longer seem important.

I have had this conversation so often that I find myself speaking in sound bites, repeating phrases I've said a thousand times before: *I am half Chinese; my mother was born in China; I spent three years living in China; yes, I speak Chinese fairly fluently, but I understand more than I can say.* I offer these words about myself to near-strangers as though they are nothing, but inside I am aware of the current that runs beneath them, the story of my language, the story of my longing. I am what I have forgotten.


The voice of my mother. The voice of my grandmother. As an infant, the first tones I heard were in Chinese. The women who held me and rocked me and sang me to sleep. Soothed by the soft murmurs of their voices, I drifted in a world without language, and yet I was already learning the sounds of Chinese. The voices of my ancestors, passing again from mother to child, rising and falling, imprinted their memory in my cells.

English, the language of my father, was also familiar to me, but it was less prominent, somewhere on the periphery, somehow more connected to the world of people who lived outside the intimacy of my home. When I started preschool I understood the language that floated around me, but I had little experience asserting myself within its midst. This world was something else, something I was a part of and yet somehow removed from. At first, my teachers were worried because I was so quiet. Then slowly I learned how to play and talk in a world of English. My teachers happily reported to my parents that I had been caught with the other girls peeking into the boys' bathroom. It was a sign of progress. But I never stopped being quiet.

At home, my mother started to speak to me in both Chinese and English, and most of the time I answered her in English. English was the language of my friends, my teachers, the books I stacked beside my bed. Chinese belonged to the private world of home, and of childhood. My Chinese vocabulary peaked when I was four. When I was eight, my grandmother moved from our home in Seattle to L.A. (to be near the rest of her children), and I spoke Chinese even less. I grew to dread the weekly Sunday night phone calls to my grandmother, ashamed of how little I could say. Afterward, I'd lock the door to my room, lie on my bed, and cry.

Language—rooted in my body, rooted in my memory. Rooted in sounds, tones, the rise and fall of meaning. The sounds of Chinese never left me. The sounds come naturally; I hear and speak their fluctuations unconsciously, like a native—it is, after all, my mother tongue. It is, and it isn't. My English is obviously far better. It is the language I learned to name my world through, the language I learned to reason and know abstract thought through. Chinese is now my second language in the sense that I am still learning it—vocabulary, complex sentences, not to mention the written characters. And yet, both languages evoke a sense of home for me. Both languages belong to me, I am both languages. I am what I speak.

I grew up in Seattle, a city with plenty of Asians and mixed-race couples. But I went to a high school that was about half black and half white; there weren't a lot of Asians, not enough that they formed any identifiable social group. Instead, social lines were mostly drawn around honors versus regular (read: white versus black) classes. Most of my friends were white, my boyfriend was white, and when I thought about issues of race and ethnicity, I thought in terms of black and white. I clearly belonged to the white side, the side that had inherited privilege and power.

It wasn't until I went off to a small liberal arts college in the Midwest that I was given the title "person of color." Surrounded by mostly white classmates, I was suddenly forced to examine myself through the lens of "other." One Sunday afternoon, I sat in a darkened movie theater in St. Paul and cried as I watched *The Joy Luck Club*. What was I doing studying Russian when the words of my own childhood language remained out of my reach? I began to study Chinese, but I had to start at the beginning since I couldn't read or write (my mother had tried to teach my sister and I when we were young, but gave up after our protests). Light years ahead of my classmates, I realized that I needed to learn by immersion.

"*Ni shi nali de?*" ("Where are you from?") In China, everywhere I went people stared at me curiously, uncertain whether I was a foreigner or Chinese. The exchange that followed was almost always exactly the same:

"*Meiguo.*" ("America.")

"*Meiguo? Ni bu xiang meiguo ren,*" ("America? But you don't look like an American.") they puzzled over my lack of blond hair and blue eyes.

"*Wo de mama shi zhongguo ren.*" ("My mother is Chinese.")

"*Ah! Guibude! Hun xue! Hun xue dou hen piaoliang. Piaoliang he congming.*" ("Ah! No wonder! Mixed blood! Mixed bloods are all beautiful. Beautiful and smart.")

I learned not to reply "thank you" to their compliments (like those thick-faced Americans), but instead shook my head and denied their flattery, or simply ignored it altogether. I'd go on to explain that my mother was born in Chongqing, but moved to Taiwan when she was three. She came to America for graduate school, where she met my father, an American, a white man. End of story. They were satisfied. I gave them the information they wanted to know. Like Americans, the Chinese were interested in what made me different, only this time it was not my Asianness that stood out, but my Westernness. I am what you want to see.

That first trip to China was only the beginning. I ended up going back many times, eventually staying for more than three years. I taught English, I traveled, I fell in love with a Chinese painter and moved into his apartment. I sank deep into a life that spoke only in Chinese. The rhythm felt natural, safe, and familiar. I knew who I was in that language, a language that triggered a whole world of cultural context. Smiling and polite, respectful of elders, humble and quiet. Perhaps this is me in either language, and yet I associate it more with the part of me that grew up in Chinese.

Only now, I was finally learning how to be Chinese as an *adult*. I devoted myself to the language, my little red dictionary and notebook by my side at all times. My vocabulary improved quickly, I inhaled new words, there was so much I wanted to say. I wanted to talk about religion, art, politics, emotions, the creative process. I wanted to share my mind, which reeled with observations and ideas, and my heart, which mourned for the silent gaps in history, untold stories—their history, my history, *our* history.

And yet, on the streets I appeared to the masses of strangers as a foreigner, as foreign as the day I arrived. It didn't take long before I grew tired of the stares, the crowds, and the oppressive pollution and density of the cities. I grew tired of constantly being on display, constantly reminded that I did not belong, no matter how fluent I became in Chinese. As time went on, I found myself increasingly starved for the part of me that spoke, thought, and breathed in English. I missed my English mind, which could choose carefully between words like *longing, hunger,* and *desire*, understanding intuitively their subtle yet crucial distinctions. In Chinese, my vocabulary was still so limited that I had to learn to live without all of these nuances of language. I missed my ability to hint at paradox—like the sense that my life was determined both by factors beyond my control and by my own free will. I also missed a certain candidness and friendliness that I began to associate with Americans. I missed the mountains and ocean and damp forests of the Pacific Northwest, I missed the coffee shops and concerts and readings and festivals, and I missed the mix of ethnicities and cultures that coexists in one country. *America*. I longed for it and appreciated it in a way that I never could have without leaving. Only in China did I realize just how American I was.

Now, back in America, my longing for China returns. Partly, it is the freedom that I associate with wandering on my own with a backpack, far from home, alive to the possibilities of each day. Also, it is what I know

now about the country: the mountains of Sichuan, the pulse of Shang-
hai, the chaos, the history, the politics, the yearning of the people—
my friends—to know and be known by the world.

But most of all, I miss living in Chinese: the opportunity to sink
down into a level of my being that was once silenced, stunted, dormant,
waiting for its chance to resurface. On a societal or political level, I am reminded of my Chinese identity every time I am the only Asian or "person
of color" in a room. But on a personal level, my sense of "being Chinese"
has everything to do with the rise and fall of the language, the soft intimacy it evokes in my voice and my heart, connected as it is to the inno-
cence of my early childhood. Back then, I knew no names or categories to
describe my identity; I simply belonged. Later, no one told me what happened to that belonging, where it went, and how I could get it back.

Who am I? What is my story? How is my story connected to my
past? What have I inherited and what will I pass on?

I am what I choose to seek.

# THE ART OF MAKING HOT TEA

## Jenny R. Sadre-Orafai

Find yourself a cup of tea; the teapot is behind you.
Now tell me about hundreds of things.

—Saki

WHAT YOU WILL NEED:
A box of Darjeeling tea
A box of Earl Grey tea
A section of the newspaper you will not read

A working stove eye
A teapot
A kettle
Water

First, you will want to mix the two flavors of tea on a section of the newspaper you never read—maybe the classifieds? Mix the flavors with your hands—you will want to do this slowly, careful not to waste one tea leaf. Once you have finished mixing the leaves together, round them up and place them in a tin that maybe you have been meaning to give back to your neighbor but never will because you always forget.

I do not remember ever really coming to any huge realization that my father was born in another country. I do remember being young and unable to spell my father's name—Yahya—my letters forever tangled. I wanted to spell "John" or "Sam"—something Western and palatable. I remember the smell of hot tea, the sound of the rattling kettle, the silver reflection of my face in the belly of the teapot. I would learn, as I got older, that tea is a means of conversation in the Iranian community. Tea brewed in the morning, in the afternoon, in the evening, and in all four seasons in my house. My father's cheeks always full with sugar cubes.

In first grade, my father came to my class dressed in his native Iranian clothing, a brown vest with squiggles of silver trim, a small sheepskin hat blocking out his thick, curly black hair, and black puffed pants. He brought *gaz*—small, white, chewy Iranian candies—for my classmates and me. He was invited to come and talk to my class about the Persian New Year, which we celebrated every year on the first day of spring. Dad was a huge hit. All my classmates thought he was extremely interesting, and while part of me was happy that everyone loved him, there was something that felt uncomfortable. Years later, I think what bothered me most was that my classmates' gaping mouths and wide eyes told me that my father was different from theirs, something that had never occurred to me before.

> Make sure to place a couple of pinches of leaves in the teapot; now set it aside. After you have done this, take the kettle and fill it three-quarters full with water from your faucet. Now, place the kettle on the stove eye. You will want to turn your heat up to seven (if ten is the hottest). Let the water boil—be patient. Maybe read the rest of the newspaper.

From the ages of three to ten, I lived in Houston, Texas. Even though Texas is unbearably hot, and even though Texans claim that the state bird is the mosquito, there is a special beauty about Houston. I remember watching the sun sink into the flat ground of our backyard; the bluebonnets growing wild along the interstate; the waves of heat creating a rippling effect through my afternoons. I felt that Texas couldn't do wrong by me.

My father and I would take winding walks in the late summer afternoons. During our walks, he would teach me numbers in Farsi: *Yek, doh, seh, chahar, panj, sheesh, haft, hasht, noh, dah.* He would teach me the words for eyes, nose, chin, and teeth. Pointing to his teeth, I would squeeze my small palms and blurt out *"Dandune."* "Very good, Jenny. Very good." And on to the next—his pointer finger on his chin. We would follow this routine all the way home, me skipping beside him.

Like that of most large cities, Houston's population consists of residents from many different parts of the country and the world. I never thought about being "other" or felt self-conscious about my looks or my long last name. I guess you could say I blended in.

Special attention was not called to my family or me in Houston; we simply went about our daily business.

When I turned ten, my father got another job in a different state. We were moving to Chattanooga, Tennessee—home of the Chattanooga Choo Choo, Rock City, and Ruby Falls. Ten was not quite what six, seven, eight, or even nine had been. I was becoming more aware of my body, my name—my identity. Suddenly I found myself in an environment that was extremely different from Houston. In Chattanooga, there was no escaping the furrowed brows during class roll call, the sudden shifting and turning of my peers as they tried hard to figure it all out—where does that name come from? How are you supposed to say it? And it was during this time that I began to go by "Jenny Sadre." I shortened my name, just as my mother, father, and sister had done. "It rhymes with padre," I would tell teachers and fellow students, and the confusion was kept at bay.

Once your water in the kettle is boiling, pour a portion of the hot water into the teapot. Place the lid on. Now, set the kettle back down on the eye and carefully take the lid off and set it aside. Take the teapot (with the lid still on) and set it down on top of the kettle. You will want to reduce the heat to maybe a four (if ten is the hottest). Let the kettle and teapot simmer.

It wasn't until I began to work on my master's degree that I became more aware of what my name meant and what I was saying to people when I shortened it. This awareness was heightened when I began work as an adjunct instructor of composition at the same institution. What would my students call me?

When I began my teaching career, I was really forced to think about my name and identity for the first time. I was well aware of the fact that by shortening my name I was making it easier on all those who addressed me. However, something kept tugging at my conscience.

My sister, Stephanie, had begun using our full last name several years earlier. I had never thought to ask her why until then. I called her.

"Hey, I have something to ask you. Why did you start going by 'Sadre-Orafai'?"

"What do you mean? Where is this coming from?"

"Well, I start school next week and I'm working on my syllabi and I don't know what to use. I feel guilty shortening our name. I don't know. Why did you start going by 'Sadre-Orafai' again?"

"I don't know, Jenny. I mean, on the one hand using 'Sadre-Orafai' helps me fit in more with other Iranians on campus. While, on the other hand, being at a place like Berkeley, I realize that difference isn't an imposition. While our name may be difficult to pronounce and uncommon, it's no more of an imposition for people to learn than 'Jones' or 'Smith.'"

I hung up the phone thinking about what my sister had said. And, when the first day of school, my first day of teaching, came around, I found myself at the front of the classroom sounding out my *entire* last name for my students—syllable by syllable. They were curious, of course, about the origins of my last name, just as my classmates had been when I was younger. But this time I simply told them.

It was also on my first day of teaching that I had something of a rude awakening. After discussing where my name "came from" and what it meant, one student said, "Wow. I really wasn't expecting someone like you." Initially, I thought she was referring to my age (at the time I was twenty-four). "What do you mean?" I asked her. "Well, I mean you don't have an accent or anything." I remember feeling the blood rush to my cheeks. She went on to explain to me that someone in the registrar's office had suggested she never enroll in a course with an instructor's name that she could not pronounce. I was shocked. As she finished, other students throughout the class nodded their heads. I asked them if they had all been told the same thing, and they had. Irate and never more proud of my last name, I asked the class if they could understand everything that

I had said, making sure that my "accent" had not gotten in the way. They laughed and said "Yes, Ms. Sadre-Orafai."

Unfortunately, that would not be the last time I would hear assumptions about my person based simply on my last name. However, I got better at handling them. I began to realize that I had been denying my heritage and, in doing so, denying my father and all my family both in the United States and still in Iran. I felt that for others to understand me, as well as what sorts of contexts I brought to situations, it was important that they know *all* of me, *all* of my name.

After I graduated and accepted a full-time instructorship at a different institution, I was given a great opportunity: to teach international students. I was thrilled. On the first day of class I told my students that I had a profound respect for every single one of them for being brave enough to come to another country, learn a different language, adapt to new customs, and enroll in college. I told them that their courage was immeasurable. And as I looked around the room at their beaming faces, faces that were growing curious as I progressed with my words, I told them that I felt this respect because, like them, my father had been an international student.

Now, as I teach my students, I can't help but think of my father and of who taught *him* composition, and of how important international students are to our schools and, more broadly, our country.

When I began teaching international students I noticed that there were many who, when I attempted to pronounce their names as my past teachers and professors had, would stop me and say, "Just call me 'Sally'" or "Just call me 'Sam.'" It was then that I realized that my students and I shared much more than my father and I did—I was more like them. "It rhymes with padre."

I often find myself engaging in discussions with my students about their given names and their "American" names. I tell them that it wasn't that long ago that I, too, Americanized my name so as to make it easier for others to pronounce. I tell them that what I call them is strictly up to them, but that I will work my hardest to correctly pronounce their names. It isn't easy working my Western tongue around names that are not as "palatable" as American names, but it is important to me that my international students know that I am willing to try to address them by a name familiar to them while they find themselves in a place not so familiar.

> Find a mug or cup—make sure it is not of the plastic persuasion. Now, take the teapot (with the tea leaves in it) and pour this concoction into your cup, filling only about one-fourth of the cup. Now, take the kettle with the water in it and pour the water into your cup until it is mostly full. Add sugar or honey for sweetening and add milk to cool off the hot tea. If, by chance, a tea leaf floats to the top of your cup, it is said by Persians that you will have a visitor at your house today.

My last name has eleven letters in it. This is because of Reza Shah. You see, to show his love for the Western world he passed laws in the early 1920s requiring Iranians to adopt last names. Up until that point, not one Iranian had a last name (or a middle name, at that). My father tells me that my great-grandfather, a Sufi, chose the last name "Sadre-Orafai"—meaning "the highest scholar."

Up until the summer of 2004, I had never seen a picture of my great-grandfather. One day in July I received an email from my father. It came with an attachment of an old black-and-white photo of a man with deep, inquisitive eyes wearing a tall hat. He looked just like my father. I pictured his forehead wrinkling, him looking around himself, looking for a last name. I imagined his voice. I imagined him saying "Sadre-Orafai." This is the name that I carry with me today and it is in this name—if you listen closely enough—that you can hear a teakettle rattle.

# Up the Mountain from Petionville: A Conversation between Two Haitian American Queer Women

Amy André and Marlene Barberousse-Nikolin

AMY AND MARLENE ARE TWO first-generation Haitian American women living in San Francisco; Amy, twenty-nine, is bisexual, and Marlene, thirty-three, is a lesbian. They got together to record a conversation—and a lot of laughter—about their experiences, similarities, and differences in growing up, coming out, and exploring multiple layers of identity.

Amy: I'll start by talking a little bit about my family history. I'm mixed-race. My dad is from Haiti, and my mother is a white American. My dad came here when he was in his early twenties, which was in the late 1960s. He met my mother here. They fell in love, and they ended up getting married after he'd been here for a couple of years. I was born a couple of years after that. It was after I was born that my dad finally got citizenship. And then my younger brother was born several years after that. So, that's my family.

Since my dad left Haiti—he left under fairly difficult circumstances, with the dictatorship that was going on at the time—he's only been back once or twice, and not for more than an extended weekend. He never really talks about Haiti; I don't know much about it. I've never been there. The majority of his siblings are in the U.S. He has a couple of siblings who still live in Haiti, but they come to Miami all the time. My family lives mostly in the Miami area and New York City. He's fairly close to his siblings.

I don't feel like I have a lot of connection with Haiti. I always got the sense that my dad was interested in his children being very Americanized. My brother and I don't speak any French or Kreyole; he's never spoken to us in French or Kreyole. So I feel like, for me, being a first-generation person, that I know more about my mother's side of the family. What I know about Haiti is mostly what my mom has told me about it. My mom went with him on one of those two trips.

Marlene: My story is a lot different. Both my parents moved here from Haiti as teenagers. I don't know a lot about my dad's side of the family, like what they were doing before they came to the U.S. They were in Africa for a little while, and then they ended up coming over here. I do believe it was for political reasons, but I'm not quite sure. On my mother's side, my grandmother moved to Puerto Rico from Haiti, then she lived in Chicago, and then she just ended up bringing over all the kids. She left her husband working in Haiti for a long time. My parents were both here in the U.S. by the time they were eighteen or nineteen years old. They met; I was born. That was in 1971.

My family is super-Haitian. I lived in Haiti for three years and went to school there. It was really great! It was probably the best time of my life, living in a country where kids have no responsibilities, other than being kids. You know, be a kid, go to school, eat your dinner, shut up! [laughter] Everybody has moved back at some point. It's such an important part of our day-to-day. A lot of my identity is wrapped up in the idea: "You're not American. You're Haitian." I fall back on that all the time, like, "Ah, I'm not American. I am, but I'm not." It was really drilled into me. I speak French, I speak Kreyole. We sat together; we had dinners together. My family is super-tight. You have to see everybody all the time.

I'm the only child that's gone away; I live on the West Coast. Everybody else is in Chicago or Miami. Even though I feel very connected to my family, I also need a lot of space from them. Sometimes I wonder if it's because I'm queer. I don't know, actually. I just know that sometimes that closeness is a little claustrophobic. My aunts talk to each other like four times a day! They're always calling . . . I go visit them and I'll say, "Oh my goodness! Do you really need to talk to your sister all the time?" But they do! They argue, they have fun. They do everything, and everything's got to be so close. I can't handle it.

My mom moved back to Haiti for a while. My dad is living in Haiti right now. He works for the Haitian embassy. My mom's back here now. She came back to help my sister with her children. I call them all the time.

Amy: My dad's side of the family is very close. He and his oldest brother are best friends. They're together all the time. They live near each other. My uncle works in my dad's office. My dad's a doctor, and a lot of the family has worked in my dad's office: my uncle, my dad's wife, my dad's wife's children. My mom helps out in his office. My mom, my dad, and my dad's wife all get along very well, better than any divorced family I've ever known, and are all close friends. There's a big family component. My dad, even though he's the middle child, is kind of the patriarch of the family, in a lot of ways. Both of his parents have passed away, and out of all of his brothers and sisters—they almost all live in the U.S.—he's the one who, I would say, has most achieved the American Dream. He went to med school, and he has a very successful medical business. He probably makes the most money, and has done the most formal education. So another thing that comes up for me is the importance of looking at class in my Haitian American family, and then class in the U.S. as a whole. My dad—yeah, he makes the most money and he's had the most schooling. But there's this automatic obligation that goes with that. He's accountable to the family. All the money is spread through the family. Everybody is working together to ensure his success, because that's part of *their* success. I don't really see that among successful Americans, in the same way. I think there is more of an individualistic mentality. I don't know if it's the same in your family.

Marlene: It is. Everybody's sort of on the same level. Leaving anybody behind is never acceptable. Everybody has to prosper if one person prospers. And there's a lot of family obligation. I don't even think about it that much. Every once in a while, I get a little freaked out, because my mom starts hinting that my sister might have to come live with me, or something like that. Because I can't really say no. I mean, I could say no. But I really can't. And I know that if I pick up tomorrow and pack my stuff up, there is always going to be a place to go. They're just always going to be there. It's very comforting, but it is a burden. Both sides of the family have seven kids. So I have the hugest family. In the immediate family, there are fourteen people right there, plus their kids, and their kids. Everybody has to look out for each other. It's a very huge thing, especially in Miami, where you know a lot of Haitian people. You have to be like, "Okay, I got a step up. Everybody, come on!"

Amy: You were born in Chicago?

Marlene: No, I was actually born in Puerto Rico. My mom was on vacation, visiting her mom, who was living there. I ended up being born there. My mother and most of her sisters were living in Chicago. I grew up there until I was fourteen, and then lived in Florida. Between seven and ten years old, I went to school in Haiti, and then came back to Chicago.

Amy: Oh yeah, a lot of Haitians here in the U.S. send their kids to Haiti for school. That happened in my family, too, with my cousins. The private schools there seem to be better than the public ones here.

Marlene: You know how the Haitians are—they send kids back for school, and also to know their culture.

Amy: I was born in New York, and I lived there until I was four. Then we moved to the islands for a couple of years. We lived in the Dominican Republic and Montserrat, while my dad was going to medical school. When I was six, we moved to Miami, where he finished medical school and became an established physician. I lived in Florida until I moved here, which was when I was twenty-two. That was about seven years ago. What brought you out here?

Marlene: I needed a change. I hate the weather in Florida. I really do! I called two friends who were in California, and it was like, whoever called me back first, that's where I was going. It was actually that easy. Within two months, I packed my stuff and left. It was just a change. It had nothing to do with my family. Now I miss them, a lot. Because it's so expensive to call! I've been out here for five years.

Amy: I grew up in Florida, and then I went to college there. And when I finished college, I came out here to San Francisco with some friends for a vacation. We did a road trip. All I knew about California was L.A. I had visited L.A. and didn't like it. But my friends said, "No, San Francisco will be different." I said, "Okay, I'll give it two weeks and see what it's like." At the end of the vacation, they went back, and I never did. I just fell in love with this city. I went back briefly to get the rest of my stuff that was in storage at my mom's house. And that was it. I thought, "This is the place for me." The one thing that I miss about Florida is the weather. I love the humidity. I miss my family, too, of course.

Marlene: Yeah! One of the things that I really miss about Miami is all the Caribbean influence. Having the Haitians, the Jamaicans, all the Caribbean people, you know, everybody's there. There's an understanding, a general understanding, that we have a very strong "other" culture. It's understood. It's not questioned, ever.

I haven't met a lot of Haitian people in San Francisco. I work at a West African restaurant, and it caters to a lot of the francophone community. There's a Haitian association that's in Oakland, so I guess there's a pocket community. But I haven't really met that many Haitian people. You know, like maybe two.

Amy: Since I've been here, over the past seven years, I've met probably about four or five Haitian people, and almost all of them are from Miami. And all of them are queer—either gay, or lesbian, or bi. That's really interesting to me, too, because when I was in Florida, I never met any queer people who were Haitian. When I came out to my dad, he told me I had one very distant cousin who he had heard was gay and lived with his boyfriend in Miami. I thought, "Right on! Awesome!" [laughter] But I had only met this guy once, when I was seven years old, so he's not someone who is in my life. So, I know that there are other Haitian people who are queer, somewhere on the planet. And then, since I've been here, I've met a few. I think it is just a San Francisco thing. If someone's gonna be here, they're gonna be queer.

Marlene: That's my theory. Everybody's queer, in whatever way, in this city. You can even be sort of hetero, but you're still queer! [laughter]

Amy: Is there a big Haitian community in Chicago?

Marlene: Yes, there really is. I grew up surrounded by Haitian people. In fact, my neighborhood was mostly Haitians and Mexicans and Polish people.

Amy: That's really interesting because my mom's family is from Poland. And she and my dad met living in the same building. They were next-door neighbors.

Marlene: I think there's a similarity between Haitians and Polish people. My first girlfriend was Polish. And sometimes I would say, "Man, you guys are just the European Haitians!" [laughter] They have similar things that they do, like the way they interact among their families, and a lot of the expectations that the moms have. The moms expect the kids to grow up and be educated, and have a career, move up in the world, make money, and take care of elders in the family. It's very similar; I think that's why they coexisted with us.

Amy: I've always wondered—because my mom's not from Haiti and has only been there that one time—what it would have been like to have both of my parents coming from the same culture. My dad was more of a provider type of a parent. I mean, both my parents worked, but my dad really *worked*. My mom took time off to have kids and was more involved in the day-to-day parenting, and my dad was in more of the money-provider role. I always get the sense that my dad grew up with the model where the women pass down the culture and do the caregiving, whereas the men do more of the traditional male things. So that was replicated in my family. But there was a missing piece, because my mom was passing down culture—but she wasn't passing down Haitian culture. She doesn't cook

Haitian food. She doesn't speak French or Kreyole. She hasn't spent a lot of time in Haiti. So, she passed on a lot about her own culture, which is a Jewish Polish culture of being third generation in the U.S. But I didn't get a sense of what my life would have been like if both my parents were from Haiti or if I had a mom from Haiti, doing those traditional mother roles. What was that like for you? Did you notice differences in your parents, in terms of caregiving?

Marlene: My parents weren't married, so I never lived with them together. My mom's not that much of a caregiver, either. But I have a family where everyone else sort of pitched in. My mom's a little wild; she's the wild child of her family. My dad was around; I saw him a lot. As I got older, we sort of rediscovered our father-daughter relationship, and we ended up talking a lot more. When I was a kid, he felt his duty was done if I was okay, had clothes on, and wasn't hungry. "You're fine! You can't complain about it." But he's mellowed out with age. He's a lot more concerned about his children. I think that change is also from living here long enough. He knows he has to be nice to us now. [laughter] Growing up within a double-Haitian family, there were always certain expectations of what the woman should do. The thing that was drilled into my head was: grow up, find a husband, make him happy, have good kids, blah blah blah. And none of us siblings and cousins have actually done that! I'm the oldest out of that crew, but none of us are really toeing the line. My younger cousins are just downright American. I almost do not see any of the Haitian influence, and I think, "Wow, I would never have gotten away with that as a kid!"

I can't say my parents were the most perfect parents in the world, in the sense of being there. But also part of being Haitian, in my family especially, is that your aunt is your mom. At one point, my mom and two of her siblings, plus all their children, were living in the same apartment building. So, you go upstairs for dinner, you come downstairs to play, you don't know where you're sleeping. Everybody's there for everyone. It's like having five moms and two dads. It's like a village. Even if everybody in my immediate family died, there would still be a whole other set of people I could run to.

Amy: My family was a little bit different. For a while, we lived in the same neighborhoods as our relatives. We lived in Miami, and my dad has siblings in Miami. But, once my dad finished medical school, which was when I was around eight or nine, my family was more into moving to the suburbs, living in a house, and eventually buying a house and pursuing that part of the American Dream. As we did that, we became more geographically distant from my aunts and uncles and cousins. I think my dad went out of his way to maintain those relationships. When we moved away from Miami and into Palm Beach County, we were interacting just as much with my mom's family; but my mom, my brother, and I were interacting less and less with my dad's family.

My parents aren't married anymore. They got divorced when I was twenty. So now when I go home to visit, I spend time in each of their houses, and my time is taken up doing that. I see my aunts and uncles even less, unless they happen to be at my dad's house. But other than seeing my dad's brothers and sisters—well, that's really my only connection to any kind of Haitian American community. I never had that sense of having multiple places I could turn to. I think that that was the deal for my dad when he was growing up, but that he wanted to create something different for his kids.

Another thing I want us to talk about is coming out in a Haitian American family, and what that was like.

Marlene: Both my parents reacted fine. My dad was great about it. He just said, "Well, you know, different strokes for different folks." My mom, on the other hand, she accepted it, but I feel like I have to come out to her again every three or four years. I'll say, "Mom, I'm still gay! I'm still queer. Please stop." Because she has her ideals of what her little girls should be, and where we should go, and all that stuff. I don't know if that's just a mom thing. But she also always respects me and the girlfriends I've brought home—which I've stopped doing! [laughter] After the last three, I realized that my mom gets a lot more attached to them than I do. When we're done, she still asks, "Where's so-and-so?!" [laughter] So now I'm like, the next one I bring over is going to have to be *the one*.

I came out when I was twenty-four. I've always sort of been the different one. So it never really surprised anyone. Pretty much all my family knows. At least, you know, my really close aunts. But then they talk so much, you really only have to tell the key person, and then it spreads. So, I'm pretty sure everybody knows. One-on-one, I have had conversations with one of my aunts, and she is probably the most understanding of all. On my dad's side, my cousin is gay, my half-sister came out to me when she was sixteen . . . so, it's prevalent. Nobody talks about it, but it's so common. I've never had any problems about it.

I know a lot of Jamaican people, and when they come out, they just have so much strife. There's such a negative view of it. I thought Haitians would be like that, but they're not. It's more like, you just don't talk about it. There's no airing out of the dirty laundry, but we all have our gay people in the family, and it's okay.

Even when I lived in Miami, I knew queer Haitians at all levels. I grew up on South Beach, so I was on South Beach all the time. So, even before I came out, I was out on South Beach, hanging out with all the queer folks. So it was just a big part of my life. My cousin came out when I was fourteen. My mom knew it. She respects him and his boyfriend.

Coming out in my family was actually pretty painless. It's also been a process. It's not like I sat the family down and said, "I'm coming out. I'm gay." So it's still a process; it's still going on right now. I've never talked about it to my grandparents. I don't know if they would care, but I don't think they really want to know what I'm doing at all. [laughter] They just say, "Okay, you're healthy! Do you want to eat? Okay, good!" [laughter] My family knows that I'm the sort of person who just really can do what I want.

It's been very easy! I was sort of upset when I came out. I really wanted to fight for it. [laughter] I really did! I was ready. And then it just ended up being like, "Oh, I'm out." And everyone else said, "We knew." [laughter] So I missed out on the great big battle!

There is a decent-sized group of queer Haitians in Florida. Just because of the vast numbers of Haitians in Florida, it's bound to happen. It was fun growing up there, in that environment.

I remember when I was young and living in Chicago, "Haitian" was a curse word. People would say, "You Haitian!" And they would talk to their little white friends like, "Oh, that Haitian!" Like you have cooties. So it was really nice to grow up, during the second part of my growing up, closer to my adulthood, in a Haitian environment in Miami, where being Haitian was perfectly fine. It sort of counterbalanced the fact that it was rough when I was a kid.

Amy: I came out to my mom when I was eighteen, and it took me another seven years to come out to my dad. Part of the reason I waited was because my dad was raised Catholic, whereas my mom is Jewish. My mom's family is very liberal, and my mom is, too. My dad was raised more conservatively. Once or twice when I was growing up, I remember hearing him say vaguely homophobic things, whereas I never heard my mom say anything homophobic. When I came out to my mom, my parents were still together. I didn't say anything like, "Don't tell Dad," but I think it was clear to her that I was just telling *her*. She was fine with it. She was more fine with it than I was. Not that I was expecting a fight. She is so liberal; I knew she wouldn't fight me on it. But I just thought that maybe it would be an event between us. I told her over the phone, and I burst into tears as I finished. She just said, "Yeah. And?" I said, "Oh, okay." And then I calmed myself down.

When I came out to my brother, he was twelve. He said, "I know lots of people who are bi." He was about to start going to a performing arts high school, which is a very queer environment. He had lots of friends who were older and were coming out. He was very precocious. Even though he was twelve, most of his friends were in their later teens. So, he was fine with it.

Around that time, when I was eighteen, nineteen, and twenty, I was thinking of coming out to my dad. I kept putting it off. I thought

I'd wait until I was in a relationship with a woman. Then I started dating this woman, and I brought her home to meet my family. But I still hadn't told my dad that she was my girlfriend. She and I didn't date very long, so I let that opportunity go.

After that, I was busy with finishing college and moving out here. I thought, "Okay, when I move out to San Francisco, then I'll tell him. Because, when I come out here, it's just going to be this big lesbian fest, and I'm probably only going to be with women for the rest of my life!" Even though I'm bi, I'm more into women. So I thought, "I'll move to San Francisco, and I'll come out to him. I'll have a wife, and I'll introduce them. Everything will be great!" And, no sooner did I get here, within a month I met this guy. We totally fell for each other and ended up getting married. We were together for a couple of years. So I thought it wouldn't make sense for me to come out to my dad, because he wouldn't really know what I was talking about. I was with a man! He loved my ex-husband. My ex-husband is from Paris, so they have French in common. They would get together and talk a mile a minute in French. They got along really well.

So there was never really a good time [to come out to my dad]. Everybody knew, including my spouse. I came out to my ex-husband even before our first date. But with my dad, I didn't think he would get what bisexuality means.

Then, the marriage didn't work out. So, after I got divorced, I thought, "I'm twenty-five, I've been planning to tell him this for seven years, and it's never been a good time. But, now that I'm done with this male-female relationship, I'm gonna do it." I envisioned that my next relationship would be with a woman, and it was. Around that time, just after my divorce, I met a woman, and we ended up being together for more than three years, which was even longer than I was married. So, once I met her, I thought, "This is it. I have to tell him because he's going to meet her. And when he meets her, I don't want it to be like, 'This is my friend!' I want it to be real." I came out to him, and it was very mild. He was in a good mood. It was right around the time that he and his second wife got married. I was in town for their wedding. I sat him down and said, "Dad, there's something I have to tell you. I'm with this woman now." He said, "Okay." And then everything was just fine.

Later, after that, she would come home with me every time I went back home. So, they ended up meeting each other many times.

My relationship with her ended about a year ago. I happened to be home again, and I told my family we broke up. He said, "Well . . . maybe you'll meet a guy!" [laughter] I think now he's getting it. He'll say, "So, what's new?" And I'll say, "Oh, I'm dating a woman, and I really like her." Even though I'm very proud and out as bi, I try not to talk so much about when I'm dating men, because I feel like he's gonna think that that means that I'm heterosexual. We've never had the "what bisexuality means to me" talk. We've just had the "I'm dating a person of this gender" or "I'm dating a person of that gender" talk. I don't feel like I'm there yet. And where that comes in with the Haitian identity is that he told me that it's not really talked about in Haitian culture. That time he told me that my distant cousin had a boyfriend, he said, "You know, we don't really talk about these things. It's okay that you do these things, but nobody needs to know about it . . ." [laughter]

When I was with my ex-girlfriend, I brought her to my ten-year high school reunion. The high school I went to was really, really homophobic. So, she and I went to Florida, to go to the reunion. We stayed at my dad's house. And, on the day of the reunion, he was getting more and more nervous. Finally, he took me aside. He said, "I'm not telling you this because I have anything against your lifestyle or your lover. Just be careful. Maybe you don't want to tell people that she's your lover. I don't want them to hurt you in any way." Given the high school, this was a real possibility. It was interesting to me because this was the first time he'd referred to her using the word "lover." Usually he would say, "Oh, your friend, your friend." And I would say, "my girlfriend." We'd had that conversation five or six times. So this time I thought, "My dad just used the word 'lover'! He's acknowledging who she is in my life!" [laughter] And he was demonstrating a real awareness of the homophobia, like an intuition of what I must have gone through. I think he knows that I was not bi starting the day I was twenty-five, but have been all along.

She and I went to the reunion as an out couple, and it was totally fine. Everyone who had been homophobic in high school outgrew it. They were just like, "Oh, cool, you're a lesbian!" I was like, "Well, actually . . ." [laughter]

Marlene: Then you have to go into that speech! [laughter]

Amy: So that was my coming-out process. It worked out just fine. I think he's getting there. I think he figured out why I moved to San Francisco. It'll be interesting to see what the future holds for us in terms of that.

Have you dated women who are also first generation or Haitian?

Marlene: My first girlfriend, which was my longest relationship, is also first generation. She's Polish. She grew up with us. She grew up in a Haitian community.

I find that people will accept me being Haitian, but also sometimes I think they consider it exotic. Like, "Oh, you're from Haiti." It becomes part of this appeal, which I really don't like.

I've never really had any problems with it with the people I've had long-term relationships with. Here I just find that most people don't have any knowledge of Haiti in general, except for the politics and anti-American sentiments that they may have heard about. When they find out I'm Haitian, they ask, "Oh, what do you think of [a current political situation in Haiti] . . . ?" It's usually not a dating question!

I've never actually dated someone who was Haitian. Even when I was dating guys, I never did. I think part of it is because I'm Haitian. I love being Haitian, but, to me, the Haitian culture itself is this gossipmonger kind of thing! Everybody's sort of interconnected. So, if you dated a Haitian boy or a Haitian girl, somewhere down the line, it's, "My mom knows your mom's best friend!" So, it was always consciously avoided: I do not date Haitians. And, you know, everybody's related! I'm sure if we sat down and really went through it, you're my cousin! [laughter] That's just how it is on an island that small.

Amy: I never have [dated a Haitian] either. My two longest relationships, with my ex-husband and my ex-girlfriend—both of them were immigrants. My ex-husband is from Paris, and my ex-girlfriend was born in Taiwan. She moved here when she was a child. So they both had the experience of being immigrants, not even being first generation. In that way, I connected with them in ways that I didn't necessarily connect with others. Also, the Haitian culture has a lot of French influence. So, my ex-husband, being French, knew a lot about Haiti.

With my ex-girlfriend, her family is Chinese, and there is a lot of similarity. There's a big focus on family connection and lots of conversation on the phone among family members. They're very loud. You go to the house, and the TV is on at full volume, the grandchildren are running around the house screaming. There's a stereotype that Asians are very quiet, and it's total bullshit! [laughter] They're screaming, just like at my aunt's house, with all my cousins, where there would be really loud people and loud music playing. It's the same in her family. They all live here in the Bay Area. So it was nice to have a family environment, where I was hearing all these languages. I didn't really know what anyone was saying, but they were all screaming it!

It reminded me of my growing up. There's a big emphasis on food, too, which also reminds me of growing up with Haitian relatives. In my mom's family, there is no emphasis on food. But in Chinese culture and Haitian culture, there definitely is.

Marlene: I've never dated any immigrants. I actually think there's a big difference between being an immigrant and being first generation. I meet a lot of immigrants, and they've grown up in other cultures and then come here; they always come here for opportunity. When you're sort of stuck here from birth, it's different. Part of me just really wants to get up and move out of here. [laughter] And I really rely on that. If worse comes to worst, I've got another country to go to! Not that Haiti's a wonderful place to be right now. But, I'd go. I think about, "What if I move over there? Where would I live? What would I do?"

People who come here on their own and for themselves have a different outlook. I'm just like, "Okay, I'd like to leave, please. Can I go?" I would love to be from somewhere else. I love Haiti! It's a beautiful— well, it used to be a beautiful place. It's gone down a lot.

My mom is from Port-au-Prince. When I go there, that's where I spend time.

Amy: That's where my dad's from. They're from Petionville.

Marlene: My family is from up the block! If you go up the mountain from Petionville.

Amy: Okay, let's wrap up. What else do you want the world to know about being a first-generation Haitian American queer-identified woman living in San Francisco?

Marlene: Being a triple minority? [laughter] I've gone through a lot of stages with my cultural identity. Probably more so than with any other identity I have. I'm at the point now where I'm super comfortable and very happy that I come from another place. I recognize that there's a difference, when I talk to African Americans in this country. I'm going to generalize, but sometimes I feel like African Americans in this country are yearning for deeper connection with their Africanness. When I meet African Americans that come to the African restaurant, they're more African than the Africans that come to the restaurant!

Sometimes I'm really happy that I have this strong culture where I can trace myself down, roots and roots down. I feel very secure. It's a racist country, but I come from a classist country. It's nice to have a really strong cultural knowledge of where you're from, and live in this country. It makes it a lot easier. If I don't like it, it's like, "I'm leaving!" [laughter] I know I can live somewhere else.

My sense of identity, as a black woman, queer, Haitian—it all really comes from the foundation of being Haitian. It's made me strong and able to deal with everything else a lot better. I don't know why. It's nice though. Okay, that's it! [laughter]

# SEX IN TRANSLATION

## Laura Fokkena

MY COUSIN AND I WERE STANDING waist-high in the lake, slowly raising and lowering our hands in and out of the water, palms outstretched, taut.

"Why do your fingers look shorter when they're underneath?" I asked her.

She slipped her hand up and down, noticing the effect, and started to say something about light and refraction, but then stopped and came up with a better rejoinder: "Maybe they really do get shorter?"

We laughed. I was eleven; she was seventeen. We'd met only twice before, on her two trips to the States. This was my first time in Germany. She was funny, just like I remembered her. She was also topless, her breasts round and full, the kind of boobs I fully intended to have if God would only answer my nightly prayers, which I offered up complete with promises to be nicer to my sister and vows to do all the extra-credit problems on my math homework if he would please, please, just fill out my bra. I was the only girl in sixth grade still wearing a 28 AAA.

"Aren't you embarrassed to take off your clothes in front of all these people?" I asked her, my eyes still politely focused on the palms of our hands, avoiding the urge to stare at her chest. I'd been thrilled when she'd invited me to the lake with her that afternoon, and positively ecstatic when we were met at the shore by five or six other students from her twelfth-grade class. *That's me, thanks, cool enough to hang out with seventeen-year-olds.* I hadn't counted on all of them getting out of their cars and stripping in broad daylight, right there on a crowded beach.

"Embarrassed?" She thought about it for a moment. I wondered if my very question had embarrassed her—I know it embarrassed me— but if it did she didn't show it. "These are my friends," she said, shrugging. "Maybe if my teachers were here or something."

She laughed at the idea of it, as though the thought of being naked in front of your teachers was so obviously humiliating it didn't merit comment. Though I could understand that much, I didn't understand why being naked in front of *everyone else in the world* was somehow okay. I wasn't naked in front of anyone, ever: not my mother, not my friends, not my four-year-old sister, nobody. Even my doctor gave me a paper sheet to cover myself with.

But I shouldn't have been surprised. For years my family had received photographs tucked in the obligatory Christmas cards featuring my German relatives naked on beaches, naked in the backyard, naked in the kitchen, naked on vacation. "Having a great time in Spain!" the note would read, and there would be one of my miscellaneous aunts with her breasts hanging out, a child or two with penis exposed darting about in a sun hat and one sandal. To be caught unawares was one thing, I reasoned, but to get such a photograph developed and think, "I must send this to my American relatives!" was another thing entirely. Who were these nudists, and how did we end up sharing DNA?

My *oma* was delighted with the pictures, had them framed, and displayed them on top of the doily that covered her television set, along-side those of her raised-in-America grandchildren wearing overcoats and snow boots.

We represented the prude contingent.


My father and his family emigrated from the North Sea village of Walle not long after World War II ended. Having lived an impoverished exis-tence in Germany both before and after the war, they saw America as a land of economic opportunity. It was agreed all around that the rest of its attractions were dubious. When I was growing up, the word "Ameri-can" was used as an insult in my family, as a way of chastising children and especially teenagers when they were insufficiently serious.

In my household, to be American was to be bloated and superficial. When my aunts and grandmother called me "American," they meant I followed pop culture and didn't know the capital of Indonesia, that I ate junk food and wore jeans and t-shirts and chewed bubblegum and was monolingual. America was an inflated military; decaying cities; sexual repression and the Bible Belt; fast-food restaurants and big gas-guzzling cars; bad slang; throngs of uneducated citizens who displayed an appalling ignorance of proper grammar (even in English! their mother tongue!); and a niece who didn't forget to turn out the lights because she was forgetful but because she was *American,* and as we all know—solemn nods around the room, please—Americans are too shallow to care about the environment. Americans, in short, were lack-ing in nuance, juvenile, and as bombastic as they were inhibited.

All children are by necessity sociologists, but those raised in immi-grant families must become anthropologists as well, since the code we follow at home rarely provides much of a guide on the street. At eleven

I wasn't interested in global energy policies or the geography of Indonesia, but the gulf between my family's European attitude toward sex and that of my American friends interested me a great deal.

In Germany I'd discovered a magazine called *Bravo*. In addition to featuring top-ten song lists and profiles of popular musicians written in a German so simplistic even I could read it, it also reliably produced at least one serious sex article per issue. These articles were accompanied by a photograph of a boy and a girl who looked like they were about to *do it*—sometimes they were on a bed, sometimes he was in his underwear, sometimes you could even see her nipples. It was all right there in a magazine that was sold in front of the counter, sans plastic wrap.

I was certain that I was allowed to purchase this smut only because my family was unaware of its contents, but when they found it hidden under my mattress their only objection was to its lowbrow reputation, not to the nudie shots. *Bravo*, they claimed, was not "substantial" reading. My father's sister, an English literature teacher at the *Gymnasium*, told me that a girl my age should be reading Willa Cather and Jane Austen novels. In her world, *Bravo* was in the same fluff category as the *Sweet Valley High* books. In my world it was something closer to *Penthouse*.

I stuffed it in my suitcase anyway, confident my friends back home would understand the significance of my find.

In America I knew that sex could be many things: exciting and dangerous, sinful and shameful, fun, mysterious, secretive, or delightful— but whatever it was, it was always A Very Big Deal. My family's banal, ho-hum attitude toward sexuality was out of place in this context, and I struggled to reconcile their casual approach to the subject with the obsessional nature of such discussions on American television, in American pop music, in American churches, and in American schools.

I received most of my cultural education from American magazines. It was through publications like *YM* and *Seventeen*—and later *Cosmo* and *Mademoiselle*—that I learned just how out of step my family's way of thinking was within mainstream U.S. culture. My aunts and cousins were comfortable with their sexuality. They didn't see their bodies as unfinished projects, and they didn't need how-to articles in glossy magazines to teach them how to be female the *right* way. In the States, on the other hand, appearing attractive and presentable took effort. A satisfying sex life was always held up as the light at the end of this tunnel, but to get there you had to suffer for it. It was almost like having a second job.

Women, I learned from these magazines, should see their bodies as works in progress. Skin should be smooth and even in tone. If you were especially light-skinned—for example, if your ancestry was so northern it bordered on Arctic—you should make use of a sunblock with an SPF of 15 or higher. (It was never too early to begin worrying about wrinkles.) Hair should be removed, except from the head—where it should be thickened through the use of either specialty shampoos or unusual grooming methods, such as brushing it upside down. Eyebrows should be pencil-thin, teeth should be whitened, eyesight should be corrected with contact lenses (*Teen* magazine explained that you could have *either* glasses *or* long hair, but not both), and the application of makeup was a science unto itself. All this and we hadn't even left the head.

The most important lessons involved weight. In America, your frame was either too big or too small, or, if average, too average. Thankfully, almost every part of the human body could be resculpted, provided you exercised due diligence. And simply exercised, period.

I should note here that in Germany, exercise meant riding your bicycle to the bakery because you were out of bread, walking up and down flights of stairs because you worked on the fourth floor of a building with no elevator, running because you were late for the bus, or planting a mammoth garden in the backyard each spring. In America, exercise meant repetitively contorting one's body in all kinds of improbable positions for the sake of repetitively contorting one's body in all kinds of improbable positions. Americans drove to their workplace, drove to the gym, ran on a treadmill like a hamster on a wheel, and then drove home. My European relatives biked to and from work and skipped the hamster-on-a-wheel bit, remaining thinner in the process. They also ate lunches filled with fresh fruits and vegetables and homemade dark bread, instead of the quick, processed meals Americans had to eat because they were so busy going to the gym. The European method secretly made more sense to me, but as my social studies teacher reminded us, America was the best country in the world, so who was I to argue?

But the main message that got through to my almost-twelve-year-old brain was this: (1) I was ugly, and (2) this was a catastrophe, but (3) it could be fixed, provided I could afford the parade of braces, lotions, creams, and waxes, and had the self-discipline to endure the regime. And I was sure that I did. I was an American, after all, of strong immigrant stock, descended from a people with a long history of pulling themselves up by their bootstraps.

Sadly, my people offered no support for my beautification plan. (In fact, if I were to be less than charitable, I would say they were downright hostile.)

"American girls have no dignity," my aunt said after I spent four hours in her German bathroom with my lotions, creams, and waxes. "American girls will do anything to please a man."

No dignity? I was offended. Hadn't she seen the effort I'd put into this project? Didn't she understand that appearing in public without even a cursory attempt to downplay your flaws and highlight your assets would do more than turn boys away—it was a breech of etiquette, a violation against the public good; almost, sort of, a sin?

No, my aunt had no awareness of this fact at all. In her mind you wore clothes that suited your personality, not your figure, and if they ended up making your shoulders look broad or your thighs look thick, so be it.

But how could onlookers tell the winners from the losers if everyone played by her rules? How could they decipher who had the most discipline, who had succeeded in the act of self-denial, and who had given in to shameful indulgences? Why, it would just be chaos.

As the day progressed, the lake filled up with other beachgoers, some, like me, tucked modestly into one-piece swimsuits; others, like my cousin, not so much. As with the photographs that graced my grandmother's television set while I was growing up, my horizon was filled with breasts and flaccid penises, wobbly knees, mothers' hips jutting out in service to their tired toddlers who needed a place to sit, and the tight, small bodies of the older children, sand pressed against their backsides. I had trouble knowing where to look, and tried to focus on the clouds in the sky. A cloud's appearance was predictable in any country.

"Jorg is the ugliest man in the world," my cousin said. "I am in love with him."

I was startled by these two statements placed side by side. If he was the ugliest man in the world, how could she love him? Didn't the one negate the other?

I understood, of course, that you had to excuse certain shortcomings in your partner. *Not conventionally attractive* I'd heard before, along with the qualifier, *But he's really nice!* I'd heard *Looks aren't everything,* and *He has a nice smile,* and even, for those who were really reaching, *What masculine hands!* But I had never heard a young woman forthrightly describe the object of her affection as *the ugliest man in the world.*

"Which one is Jorg?" I asked.

She pointed. She was right. He was, in fact, the ugliest man in the world. Had he been American, his parents would have assessed the situation as he approached adolescence and taken control of the matter. Orthodontia would have been procured, dermatologists consulted. As it was, Jorg just *existed* in all his goofy ugliness, comfortable under his ludicrous haircut, casual in the awkward slope of his spine. His appearance was oddly compelling, if only because it was so unusual. I couldn't stop looking at him.

"I am in love with him," my cousin repeated.

It had never occurred to me that being unattractive could be just a *characteristic,* like being tall, or knowing how to juggle. In America the word "ugly" was the mother of all insults, the Worst-Case

Scenario. My cousin's attitude made all my efforts to alter my body seem almost . . . optional.

I didn't know what to make of this.


"I don't understand," Gunda said, her English betraying just a hint of an accent, "why you can't just be forward with someone. If I'm interested in him, why can't I just tell him so? Why do I have to be so mysterious about it?"

The wine was almost gone. More than twenty years had passed since that first summer I'd spent in Germany, and my cousins and I, now in our early thirties, were attending a family reunion in a hotel next to the Mississippi River. Gunda had been raised in Germany but had moved to the States as an adult. Growing up, she had been my same-age counterpart across the ocean, the one my *oma* had always compared me to, although we didn't spend much time together until we were both in high school and began traveling back and forth every summer.

Gunda was now toying with the idea of beginning a new relationship with an American man, but was irritated by the lengthy process involved in getting things off the ground. My sister and I plied her with advice, writing and rewriting possible scripts for her to use.

"Tell him this," we suggested, or, "No! Say it this way. Then if he says this, you can say that, but if he answers this other way, you would come back with—"

But Gunda wasn't having it. She found the process exhausting, barely worth the trouble. I couldn't blame her. I found the conversation itself exhausting, although it was one I'd been having with my female friends since elementary school and one I really should have been used to by then.

A few weeks earlier, I'd read a guidebook for foreigners who were working in the United States. It quotes a Polish woman who said that she'd never realized she had to do anything special to be considered feminine ("Isn't being a woman enough?"). The author explains that self-improvement is a major theme in American culture. Given the attention Americans devote to their lawns, their home decor, and getting the next promotion at work, it is no surprise that American women devote a great deal of time to making themselves appear more youthful and more attractive, and that they approach the art of flirtation with the same serious attitude, even as they take pains to come off as breezy or coquettish. To do anything less—to just *show up*—would be seen as laziness, and laziness is considered a major personal shortcoming in the United States.

How to explain this to someone who hadn't grown up here? I probably didn't need to. Gunda had lived in the States long enough, and I suspected her question was rhetorical. But the exchange made me rethink my own background.

My American friends often joked that I was too nervous or too embarrassed to talk about sex, and in the interest of politeness I'd heard them out, but I wasn't really convinced. Sexuality conversations in America tended to pit the Catholic nun against *Playboy* and *Hustler*; situated Phyllis Schlafly opposite Susie Sexpert. This was the schizophrenic version of the world I'd studied and assimilated growing up, but as I sat there talking to my cousin about her boyfriend woes I realized I'd never really lost the part of me that made me European.

When I was fifteen I'd written a series of articles for my school newspaper about your classic Serious Subjects, the ones I'd seen in all the teen magazines I'd so earnestly studied back in junior high—drug use, rape, abortion, birth control. One time I went to Planned Parenthood and pretended to need a pregnancy test, then went home and wrote up an account of the experience. I won awards for that piece (and my journalism advisor got angry letters from concerned parents in my town), but when I showed the article to a girlfriend in Germany a few months later, she only remarked on the fact that I'd written that I was "nervous."

"You mean you weren't just cool about it?" she asked. She didn't understand all the hoopla anyway. It was a teenage girl going to a women's health clinic. So what?

I felt that familiar pang of embarrassment, one that had nothing to do with sex and everything to do with my place in life as a halfie who stood between two cultures, one foot on each side of the Atlantic, forever afraid of missing social cues. I wanted to explain to her the significance of this article, but to do that I would have to first explain the history of Christianity in the United States, quote statistics on teenage pregnancy, tell her of the politics behind discussions of birth control and abortion, and try to convey the odd place American teenagers occupy on the child-adult continuum.

So, "Yeah, I dunno, it was weird," I mumbled, shrugging it off, regretting that I'd even showed her the piece in the first place. I slid the article back into my clipbook and we went back to watching TV, where a dubbed version of *Dirty Dancing* was playing on her brother's VCR. She didn't understand the controversy around that, either.

What my American friends didn't understand was that I didn't fear talking about sex so much as I feared coming off like one of the adolescent boys with underdeveloped shoulders in a John Hughes movie, leering at girls in a locker room, which is pretty much how all American discourse involving sex and body image was described by my friends and family members in Germany: puerile.

I appreciate many things about the United States. I like jazz and blues, the vastness of the Western landscape, being able to go shopping on a Sunday, and the fact that Americans don't refer to third-generation immigrants as "guest workers." I like the easy acceptance of new ideas in this country, love Americans' flexibility and their wide-eyed lack of pretension when they travel, even though I know it makes them—us—the butt of many jokes. I especially enjoy discussing politics with Americans. They're willing to dig deep for the root causes of injustice, rather than attributing all of the world's ills to apathy and ignorance, the way so many of my German relatives do.

But I sometimes wonder how my life would have gone had I grown up in Europe. In the last course I took before graduating from college, we discussed research that showed that girls' academic performance in the United States dropped off at around ninth grade. It was a phenomenon that had been documented over and over again, a trend that was attributed to adolescent girls' sudden desire to become sociable, popular, and nonthreatening.

My classmates argued back and forth. Many were unconvinced by the fundamental premises of such research; others wanted to know why it mattered so much if girls wore a little lipstick and skipped a couple of math classes. It's not like the world was going to grind to a halt if Maggie and Caitlyn preferred cheerleading to calculus. A few argued that maybe girls really do get dumb once they hit fourteen. It was probably genetic. What kind of a man-hating feminazi would even conduct such a study in the first place? Tempers flared.

A young woman in the back of the room, pretty, with a long brown ponytail, timidly raised her hand. When my professor called on her the room fell silent; she'd barely said a word during the entire semester, and we couldn't help wondering what had finally moved her to speak up.

"If this hadn't happened to me in high school," she said, shaking the pile of papers in front of her, the research that documented girls' slide into uncertain passivity, "my whole life would have been different."

There was dead air for several seconds.

It was such a simple statement, but it stopped me cold.

Everyone, the world over, tells you to *be yourself.* But what does that mean? Your "self" is an organic concept, one that shifts and changes with geography and circumstances. We act as though we are immune from cultural influences, particularly if we are American, citizens of a country that exalts the rugged individualist.

But I thought back to the four hours I'd spent in my aunt's German bathroom with my lotions, creams, and waxes, and my awkward attempts to brush my hair upside down. I thought about the time I'd wasted ensuring that my legs were perfectly smooth and that my eyebrows resembled spermatozoa, the money I'd spent on gym memberships instead of travel, and the books I hadn't read because I was too busy worrying about wrinkles back when I was eleven years old. I thought about the mystique surrounding sex that U.S. culture treats as universal, inherent in the subject itself. I wondered what high school would have been like for me if I hadn't been consumed with efforts to fit in or (on the days when I dressed strangely) to defend my right to deviate.

"But you're here," my professor said to my classmate. "You've done well, made it to this university . . ."

The woman shook her head, adamant, and said it again: "My whole life would have been different."

# THE LATINA IN ME

## Rosie Molinary

THE LATINA IN ME IS FRUSTRATED. She stays awake late and contemplates marriage and feminism while my *gringa* sleeps. I never fought this battle before, not until my friends started marrying and producing children, and my Latin mother started suggesting marriage to the man I consider her Great White Hope.

Mamacita has been praying for a husband for me for far too long. She lights candles and recites rosaries for her *hijita soltera*.

"Don't ask for an *esposo* in my name," I implore.

"¿*Y qué?*" she replies.

"Pray for starving children. That's the type of prayer for which you call upon God. Do that in my name."

"*¿Oh sí?*" she challenges, and I see I have done nothing to alter her agenda except add a whispered postscript for good measure to make this *hijita* less of a spitfire *y más feminina*.

I figure it goes like this: I, the multicultural child of Latino parents and American upbringing, should be able to take from my culture what I want and then add anything else as I go. A little bit of MTV here, some pizza there, football on Thanksgiving, winter flurries, a lifetime without dresses or makeup, and dating early without the parental inquisition. Throw that all in with the Taina in me: loud music, spicy foods, long embraces, energetic dancing, decibel-shattering Spanish-language conversations, and an extended family tree, and there you find me, as Americanized as the Native Americans: colonized, yet fighting the conqueror.

But then, that was me figuring it out nice and neat and convenient, and the one thing I've learned in this America (which any good old boy will gladly remind me is not mine to claim) is that there isn't much here that is nice and neat and convenient, and my ethnicity has affected my self-concept too much for me to ignore it. The Latina in me finally has to make peace.

Mamacita wants me married. We both ignore this truth as if it might somehow be less apparent the more it's downplayed. I am wrecked not just by her idea that marriage will be my salvation, but by the hope that it will give her, an assurance that marriage and children will make me the Latina that I have never been. I am too certain for her taste, too independent. I try to ignore her disappointment in my casual appearance, my autonomy, my dismissal of the importance of men, marriage, and children. She will not accept that my desire to take care of myself is not to spite my Latin culture; it is not an indication of my Americanness; it is not a blemish in my character.

I feel this way, but then I consider the Americans I know, and how most of them see me as one of them, and I am stuck, stranded, struggling to figure out how I became an Anglo without any birthright. Ultimately, with the dismissal of my otherness, I stifle my voice.

I have always faltered in conversation, struggled with what I want to say and what I cannot say. As a first-generation Puerto Rican girl in the American South, I never found company for reflection. It began at home, where I did not have the Spanish words to explain to my parents what it meant to be seen as un-American when my citizenship was just as valid as that of the towheaded boy sitting next to me in social studies. He didn't agree, and he spat at me later, phlegm and hatred wrapped in one. I shook as I confronted him, terrified that I would not find the words to tell him that I had worth, that I did not belong working in his kitchen, that I could participate in his world, or any other that I chose. I told myself that I had done the right thing, that my words had been right, and that the world was, indeed, open. But I had no one to talk to who might understand. I had learned English in school and Spanish at home, and there were multiple words, understandings, ideas that did not intersect. How could I come up with the word for *racist* to explain this solitary experience when my parents had never mentioned the word or the idea? I had no one to talk about it all with, and I struggled to discover when and how to offer my voice.

Not until those preteen years did I begin to understand that because of my skin tone, I might be categorized without my consent. In the dark and musty hallway of my school one day in sixth grade, I stood fumbling with my locker. My usually pale olive skin was tan from the summer. My black hair hung over my eyes. As I wound the lock back and forth, a girl with a long and wild rat tail candidly asked, "Are you mixed?" I struggled to understand what she meant, how she might see me as "mixed." She reworded her question: "Is your daddy black and your momma white?" In South Carolina in the mid-1980s, heritage mattered as much in friendship as kindness and decency.

I explained about Puerto Rico, our homeland in the Caribbean. She stared at me, vacant and dissatisfied, willing me to stop speaking so that she could offer what she thought.

"You gotta be one or the other, white or black. I'm just gonna call you white 'cause you're smart."

That was that. She closed her locker, walked off content, and later even asked me to spend the night at her house. The exchange was complete for her and numbing to me. I had no desire to be white in her eyes, or in anyone else's. I wanted my own definition, wanted to be seen in the way that I saw myself: as a first-generation Puerto Rican trying to pave her way.

As I got older, the number of unpleasant truths I had to keep from my parents grew. At first, people denied my heritage because they did not understand my ethnicity. Later, people denied me opportunities because they felt that they knew my ethnicity better than I did.

In immigrant families, children often play the role of parent as their parents struggle to learn language and culture while simultaneously providing for their families. Children's adaptability allows for a more rapid assimilation and language acquisition. This comfort in the new country quickly yields them adult responsibilities in protecting the family. I worked hard to protect my parents from the negative elements of America that I was experiencing. I wanted them to feel satisfied with their decision to stay in the States. I wanted to keep the suitcases from coming off the shelves, the FOR SALE signs out of the yard. I *wanted* America, the only home that I could remember, despite the fact that not all of her people wanted me, so I learned to protect my parents from what no one wanted to believe could happen here.

I never told my parents about the guidance counselor who reviewed my perfect report card and wanted to remove me from honors classes and enroll me in Work Readiness courses. My file differed in only one way from those of my peers in the Talented and Gifted program: It read "Puerto Rican."

Shocked, I left his office and stumbled down the hall, my red face drawing the attention of another counselor, who knew that I had potential and added me to his own caseload. Years later, he encouraged me to apply to a number of colleges and to ask for waivers of the application fees. "Let's see how we can do," he smiled as I nodded, and my Latina took on the challenge, fueled by a desire to prove that first counselor wrong.

When I wasn't being judged for my ethnicity, I was being denied it. In English class, I was told by a fellow student that I was *not* Puerto Rican, because I was not like the other Puerto Ricans, because I was neither pregnant nor strung out like the "Reekins" that this girl knew. In her world, if I didn't have track marks, I couldn't be from the Caribbean. My face grew hot as I argued, and the anxiety that had visited me years earlier with the spitting boy, the rat-tailed girl, and the narrow-minded counselor haunted me again.

This denial rendered me silent, frozen on the border between my Latina and my *gringa*, wondering which face to look to or turn from in order to find myself. In college, a friend denied my ethnicity as we talked about my upbringing. We were discussing the rules in my family based on God, culture, and machismo. "You are not a *gringa*," my mother would tell me after she forbade me to sleep over at a friend's house or cruise the mall. I would shuffle back to the phone, trying to figure out how to explain what I considered irrational reasoning to my friends; I did not want them to dislike my parents. My college friend eyed me as I told this story.

"But you aren't really Puerto Rican," she insisted.

Why did she believe this so absolutely? How could she determine what made up my whole? How was I betraying my truth?

Those were the things that used to keep me silent. I believed that no one wanted to hear what I had to say, and so I never said it. My parents couldn't understand what I had to say, so I never explained it. Ultimately, I learned that the issue is more often about vision than about words. It is about how people define what they see, and how I see myself.

When I walk New York City streets (the one place where a young man has screamed out, "Hey, *Boriqua,* over here"; where my Puerto Ricanness has never failed to be recognized; where I am still not certain that I am Latin enough; and where the random greetings from my homeland leave me simultaneously thrilled and intimidated), I see women who've bought into the myth about our sexuality. They are riveted by the fixed illusion of what being a Latina might mean.

"It means nothing," I want to shout.

But that's not true. There have been times when it meant too much to me, and I cannot escape those memories, so I swallow my words and keep company with my Latinness.

I started college with black hair, full lips, and round breasts nervously packaged in a suntan and lip gloss, distinctly different from most of the blond, reed-thin, affluent, and stylish women on campus. I met Christopher within weeks of my arrival. He approached me one evening after a meeting on community service opportunities, and we were both captivated. I learned later that he shared my Puerto Rican heritage and Southern upbringing. He was tougher than most guys I knew, and the toughness intrigued me and brought out my own edge. Because I was petrified by what I felt and acutely aware that falling for him would mean I would have to make tough decisions about privacy, intimacy, and sexuality, I pretended to care less for him than I really did.

In a friend's dorm room one Saturday night, I found myself alone with Christopher.

"Hey, girl." He moved toward me, and I looked at him shyly. My eyes tracked over his caramel-colored skin, chocolate brown eyes, and ebony hair, and lingered on the mole on his face.

He slipped his fingers under my chin and tilted it toward him. I closed my eyes for a moment and then reopened them to find him pressing toward me, surprising me with one of many kisses that I would replay for years. We would argue about this kiss for the rest of our friendship, the question of who kissed whom never settled.

"Come out with me," Christopher pleaded, and in that moment, our pattern was born. I wanted nothing more than to be out with him that night. But it terrified me, too, the list of possibilities such a decision would create. I thought that Christopher and I were mismatched, and so I didn't try to match him, despite our affection for each other.

I clung to the myth that I had of myself as a sweet, innocent, impassioned girl, which was central to my self-understanding. It was who I allowed myself to embody. Calling on that girl became a habit of mine that emerged in many potential relationships after him.

"I can't," I whispered, placing my hand on his arm and then slowly backing away. My fingers touched the inside of his forearm as long as they could before the distance became too much.

Over the years, I battled this intense attraction. I wanted him desperately, but I was terrified of that wanting, unsure of what it meant and how to control it if I unleashed it. I was willing to take barely any physical or emotional risks with him. We kissed in private places, and then I'd casually walk away. He shared intimate details of his life that he had never told anyone. I could rarely match his candor. I was terrified of being direct, of telling him what I felt, of being vulnerable. Early on, he sensed my withholding, both physically and emotionally, and confronted me one summer as we worked together in Puerto Rico in a program for orphans.

"Why are you so damned closed?" he yelled as we walked on the beach, our workday in Puerto Rico done.

I couldn't answer him, my pace speeding up and taking me away from him. If I opened myself up to him, really let him have my heart, could I ever get it back? And would I be the woman that he thought I was? Would I be good enough to have him forever? Could he love both my *gringa* and my Latina in the measures in which they appeared? Could I love whatever woman I was in his company?

Our world operated in the shadows of night, and I saw the women he was with in the daytime. I felt smaller than them, sweeter, too clean-cut, too plain. I couldn't imagine him dating someone so inexperienced, and yet, each time that I was with him in private, I came to defy my understanding of myself.

Over the three years we shared together at college, I became confident and sexy. We studied together, and I would suddenly kiss him. He'd ask about other dates, and I'd blow him off. On long car rides through the countryside that surrounded our campus, I would tenderly stroke his hair. Back on campus, I would kiss him in the parking lot and then jump out of the car, head to my dorm without looking back. In some weird twist of fate, I replaced the toned-down parts of me with more apparent traces of my Latina nature. We both grew to love this woman who was sassy, fun, and confident, and he wanted as much of her as he could get. I did, too.

We never dated, as much as we watched each other across rooms, took long drives, and spilled secrets, called each other from foreign countries, visited across state lines; we never made our relationship official. But over time, he made me believe that there was something infinitely sexy in the way I worked ceaselessly for my passions, in my Puerto Rican heritage, in my pseudo-edge and confidence, in my self-sufficiency and independence.

He moved on through women I considered needy, and I wondered, afterward, if I had gotten it right. Clearly the edge had not won him over, and, while he had found it attractive, he had not found it compelling enough.

He asked once, "What if we had ever dated? Could we have made it?"

I paused before I answered, knowing that no matter what I said, we could not get our history back. I would never feel his hand on the small of my back again, guiding me through a room and telling me how beautiful or intelligent I was. We wouldn't kiss in inappropriate places, at inappropriate times, anymore.

I stared at him, horrified that I might reveal the depth of my affection for him.

"We wouldn't have made it. You need someone who is higher-maintenance than me."

I walked off before I could hear him say, "You're right."

He had always fallen for women who needed him, who defined themselves through him. I did my own maintenance. I felt that I had no needs to be met by someone outside myself when, really, I was just beginning to understand boundaries and react to them. I was so sturdy, so rational, so stable. Romantic passion was not any of those things, and that frightened me.

I coached myself to compete in his world, to go match for match with him. While I didn't need him to define me, I was no more self-sufficient than the woman he would end up loving, but I had strapped on such severe Latinness with an American flair that he could not detect my fault lines. But in strapping on that person, I became her, a more confident, defiant, up-front girl on her way to womanhood. He forged the metal to my steel-wool edge, made me brave enough and strong enough to alter how I approached the world—but, ironically, for us to have made it, I would have had to have learned bravery *before* he helped me acquire it.

Later, the Latina mystique chilled me most. Some men find me sexy and beautiful, alluring and free game, not because I *am* those things, but because I am ethnic, a girl from the island, a Latina who must be able, they think, to make love in a whole new way.

In my twenties, as a teacher who embraced modesty, I wore long skirts and baggy sweaters, and nevertheless elicited sexual reactions from students when I mentioned my ethnicity. At twenty-two, on my first day with a new class, a group of boys slapped high fives and affectionately started calling me their "Puerto Rican Pecan." As in, "Man, our Puerto Rican Pecan makes me want to blow a nut." It stunned me, numbed my understanding of my ethnicity, made me wonder if I should go on embracing my roots or ignore the part of my identity that might make me seem sexy instead of intellectual.

As I became a more bold authority figure, I learned I sometimes had to shield from my students the side of me that was hip, young, and vibrant. What was it about me that made my students cross the line? Why did my students look me up and down, ask me to the prom, inquire about my private life, wonder aloud if I was sleeping with the soccer coach? What was it about me that was so sexual to them when my own life seemed so asexual?

As a teacher, I wanted to claim my ethnicity in order to empower my students to celebrate their own heritages. I could "pass" as white, but I had never wanted to, and, finally, I thought that I controlled a forum where, with my lead, nobody would have to pass. We could all just be who we were.

Maybe my idealism fell short. While my students did not buy into the more negative stereotypes that my peers had when I was in school, they had different opinions of what being a Latina might mean. In the teachers' lounge, I swapped stories with other young, single teachers. These women were attractive, intelligent, fun-loving. They never mentioned their students propositioning them. I came to interpret the line of delineation as based on race. My colleagues were white, my students African American. In my students' eyes, I represented two things: the crossroads between the white and black worlds and a local version of the sexy women that they lusted for in hip-hop videos filmed on location across the Caribbean.

It was as if my Latinness insinuated sensuality and sexuality. I was a myth and not a woman, Wyclef Jean's Maria to all these wannabe Don Juans. It seemed that my womanhood meant sex and sensuality more than any other woman's, as if I could simply exhibit my breasts and never my mind and no one would be the lesser for it, as if by my very ethnicity I was promiscuous and uneducated, as if I had been created merely to procreate.

For years, I was unable to accurately perceive myself because I was waiting for that accuracy to come from someone else. I was waiting to always be a Latina or always a *gringa*, to always be pretty or always be plain, to be exotic or ignored, to be exciting or unappealing. I wanted a constant but I never found it. The reactions to me were always extreme. I was waiting for external consistency to bolster my own confidence. Ultimately, I realized that the only consistent view that I would ever get would be my own. My glance in the mirror would have to be accurate. I would have to respect my own assessment. My self-confidence would teach others how to interpret me so that I did not have to make any sacrifices. The most important thing was not how other people defined what they saw, but how I defined what I felt, the way I melded my parts, and, thus, how I let my Latina and *gringa* each have her own voice.

Maybe, here, I find the root of my fear of marrying: this idea that with marriage I might finally become something that fits into a box of understanding. In the past, I could never be just Puerto Rican because it rivaled what others defined as Puerto Rican, but I could also never be just a white or black girl because I defied those definitions as well. I was a shape-shifter, transcendental, a mirage. And now I have fallen in love with the not-belonging, the mystery, the freedom from place. But what if marrying changes all that, gives me a club, the way my mother hopes that it might? What if marriage precludes place and leaves me stranded in a one-dimensional world of "wife," far less vast, rich, and decadent than the lives I have been able to try on until now?

There is my fear: I will sacrifice my identity in marriage. The price of the union will be me. I do not want to become a full-time cook, maid, chauffeur, and beauty queen. I hate that the Hispanic formula of femininity, coupled with the cult of domesticity, makes some women into pawns who have no idea what hit them, or that they've even been hit at all. I imagine that is why my Latina is awake way past midnight, and my *gringa* sleeps soundly through this inner turmoil. The Latina, a Latina cut from a different cloth than the one my *mamacita* would like me to try on and from a different cloth than my teenage students think they know, is keeping vigil for the next life to come. What will this woman allow for me, she thinks? Will others keep missing me when they look in my face, or will I finally be recognizable?

It seems, lately, that *la isla* is barreling down on my American upbringing as if it might be the end. Get a diamond ring on her finger, my mother must be thinking, and she'll come back to our team. But I am not the standard *gringa* nor am I the traditional Latina and, finally, I know how to unite my soul.

I am the union of my parts. The truth is that every woman can be saccharine and salt, beauty and brawn, gentle and razor sharp. The wedding ring, Mamacita, changes nothing that I don't want it to change. From the very beginning, I had it right. I, the multicultural child of Latino parents and American upbringing, am able to take from my cultures what I want.

# KIMIKO

## Melissa Secola

"WHAT ARE YOU?" HE ASKED, STUDYING ME as though I were some exotic species of wild white orchid. Truthfully, there was nothing romantic about his gaze. He eyeballed me the way one might eyeball mystery meat soaking in tepid mystery-meat juice. "Half Japanese, one-quarter Swedish, and one-quarter Norwegian," I answered. "But I have an Italian last name. It's a long story," I continued, despite his quizzical expression.

My roommate's boyfriend was an ex-marine with an aging crew cut and a Kewpie-doll smile. He spoke with a Southern twang and used words like "fixin'" and "yonder." Aptly, he was named Dallas. He swept up a handful of confetti from the night before and suddenly looked at me. I watched his face as the concept of my being multiracial finally registered, and he gleefully exclaimed, "You're a mutt!"

The postmodern, politically correct world stood still a moment as the weight of his sentence crushed me. I felt a pain in my chest, the kind of dull but startling pain you feel when you remember the terrible thing someone once said about you in the eighth grade. His three words transported me back to childhood, to a time when I felt split between two worlds and afraid of breaking if I didn't bind them together. All my life I had been asked, "What are you?" The guesses were numerous, exasperating, entertaining, and always wrong. "Mexican?" "Spanish?" "Italian?" "Indian?" My personal favorite: "Are you an Eskimo?" And then there was the safe guess: "European?" There were people I had known for years who still called me Chinese. But I had never before been called a dog.

I looked in the mirror. I had freckles and small eyes and a Nordic nose. I was tall and slender, with fingers as long as E.T.'s. I was like an impressionist painting that everyone interprets even though the details are fuzzy and the colors bleed together. People assumed I was subservient upon learning that I was half Japanese; strangers in grocery stores confided in me their prejudices against "Orientals" when they were unaware of my roots. I looked again at my reflection. I saw that I was different. I was a puzzle with jumbled pieces. I was mystery meat . . . the kind we used to buy at Happy Hamburger when I was a kid.

"Did you say 'One Happy Special with orange sauce?'" the drive-through voice asked with contempt. My mother leaned out the car window a bit.

"No, I said, 'Two Happy Specials, no orange sauce.'"

"Excuse me?" the voice demanded.

"I said, 'Two Happy . . .'" my mother began.

"Excuse me? I can't understand you," the voice interrupted.

"TWO HAPPY SPECIALS, NO ORANGE SAUCE, PLEASE!" I articulated from the backseat. I turned around and stared at the long line of cars forming behind us.

"Five-twelve at the first window," the voice droned.

Growing up, I never liked the drive-through at fast-food restaurants. I didn't like the tight bend our car had to turn before getting to the pickup window, or the outdoor menu where meals were designated by numbers and vague adjectives: #5 Happy Special Combo. I didn't like the way they spelled it: drive-*thru*. Most importantly, I didn't like her accent . . . my mother's.

My mother moved to America when she was twenty-six years old. She had never before been outside of Niigata, a Japanese town known for its rice and sake, and while she'd loved going to the American cinema every Friday night with her friends, where they watched movies starring John Wayne dubbed into Japanese, she didn't dream of America. She liked the confectionary shops that made *shu cream*, Japanese cream puffs, and *omochi*, soft globes of sweet rice with red beans in the center. She liked the cherry blossom trees in the park near her apartment. And she liked *ofuro*—deep bathtubs—and tatami floors. Then one day she fell in love with my father, a young American stationed at the naval base. After four years, they married at city hall in Tokyo and moved to America. Over the years, my father taught my mother English. He also taught her not to noisily slurp the noodles in soup, an eating habit customary at the noodle shops in Japan, and that the clocks must be changed during daylight saving time, a concept that she refused to believe until she checked the clocks in at least three stores on Main Street. She taught him to take his shoes off before entering the house.

My father studied at New York's Culinary Institute, while my mother stayed home and took care of me. We lived in a house built on top of a wine cellar in a small town in Dutchess County. There were many Italian Americans and conservative housewives, but very few minorities; my mother's weekly visits to the grocery store certainly widened the eyes of an otherwise sleepy town. After a few years, my father moved us to the West Coast, where the roads seemed as endless as the ocean they ran alongside, and the people were more diverse. My parents bought their first new car, a red Volkswagen, right before my younger brother was born, and they dreamed of someday buying a house. My mother hoped for wood floors, and I hoped for a big backyard.

After my father became a chef, things slowly began to deteriorate. His place at the dinner table was often empty, yet my mother continued to set the table for four, even washing his unused plate at the end of the meal. I remember hearing keys jangling at the door on the nights that he came home late. As he crept through the hallway, a strong, rancid smell followed. The sound of attempted quiet was like the unsettling calm before a bomb explodes—in this case, the loud thud my father's body made as it collided with the wall and slumped to the ground. The next morning, he'd be gone, like some terrible nightmare you awaken from. I secretly wished he wouldn't come home at all, and pretty soon, he didn't.

By the time I was a teenager, he had disappeared. Ten years would pass before he resurfaced in my life, his addiction, like a tornado that ripped through us, finally over. All that remained of my parents' life together in the ruins we called our home were pictures stored in tattered cardboard boxes in the closet: pictures of the red Volkswagen, of my younger brother and me, of them in Japan from what seemed like a lifetime ago, when they were young and happy. When my father left, he took the red Volkswagen, leaving my mother with the little red Radio Flyer wagon, which she used to transport my brother around town while I walked alongside them. Without my father, she was a foreigner, a true foreigner. The day he left, I became my mother's lifelong confidante, interpreter, and backseat accomplice at the drive-through.

There weren't many Japanese people in our town. It was the type of place that held a festival in honor of a vegetable every year, the type of place where migrant workers with placid expressions rode their bicycles to work every day. We lived in a small rented house with green carpeting. It wasn't emerald green or forest green, but green like the inside of an avocado with yellowish-brown bad spots. I grew up hearing my mother's Buddhist chant every afternoon after school. I grew up thinking that eating fermented soybeans was normal. And I grew up knowing that trips to Happy Hamburger were a small feat. There was a hot breakfast on the table every morning, never cold cereal, and my childhood was not without a sort of warmth created by my mother. But still, a great, cold fear loomed over us. I remember hiding in my closet whenever the doorbell rang soon after the first of the month, the big, booming voice of our landlord, Mr. Smythe, sure to follow, asking for the overdue rent check. I also remember the day my mother accepted a block of government cheese from the truck that stopped at the community center on Tuesdays. On tuna casserole nights, the slowly shrinking industrial-size block, wrapped in shiny tinfoil, would appear on our counter, as glaring as the look of shame on the faces of the people who stood in line to receive theirs. We never took a block of that cheese again.

With two young children and English as her second language, my mother didn't consider college an option. Instead, she worked three different jobs, all involving manual labor: She washed silk napkins soiled at weddings, stuffed yarn into sewing kits, and put snaps on baby carriers after she got home. Then she'd make dinner, insisting the meal include a fresh vegetable, never canned. She'd ask me about my homework and look greatly pained when she didn't understand or was unable to help me with a book report. She made us promise to do well in school. She told us how important it is to have a home of your own. From an early age, I began to have big dreams, dreams that didn't include green carpeting or government cheese. I focused all of my energy on doing well in school, saving my babysitting money, and finding a life much grander than the one I had. My concerns were like any other twelve-year-old, only my concerns had little to do with school dances or jean skirts or the mall. And then one day it seemed as though I were transformed from a twelve-year-old into a self-centered, insecure, blemished, know-it-all miniature adult. I was thirteen, I had a love/hate relationship with Happy Hamburger's twice-dipped fries, and the last thing I wanted was to be different.

That summer, I sprayed the entire bottle of a two-dollar product called "Sun Kissed Locks" on my hair with the hope that I would become a blond. My hair turned green. I was only thirteen, but I felt like I was leading a double life, like the Incredible Hulk. There were even times when I wasn't sure who I was. I hid my Japanese culture from my friends and glamorized my father when they asked about him. I showed them old newspaper clippings of him, the once-brilliant chef, while I secretly wondered what his favorite sandwich was. Did he like cream cheese and jam sandwiches like me? My friends never saw me as anything other than what I wanted them to see me as . . . one of them. Then one day I made the mistake of inviting Susie Thomas over to my house. Like me, Susie was a self-centered, insecure, blemished, know-it-all miniature adult. She was also popular and the biggest gossip in the eighth grade.

As we stepped through the front door, Susie tripped over about fifteen pairs of shoes, meticulously lined up in the entryway like a brigade of little soldiers. Just as she recovered, I noticed a couple of women bustling through our kitchen with platters of food. An overly garlicky smell wafted by us. "What's that smell?" asked Susie. "What smell?" I asked as a platter of *gyoza*, Japanese dumplings, sailed past me. The foreign words and voices coming from our kitchen became a cacophony of sound, noise to some perhaps, but as familiar as my own voice to me. I spotted my mother near the sink. "Mom, what's going on? I invited Susie over. I thought we could watch a movie and order a pizza." My mother turned to me and said, "We're having a meeting." *Meeting.* I knew what that word meant, and it did not involve people sitting around a table in a fluorescent-lit boardroom with pads of paper and a box of glazed donuts. I looked at the collection of shoes, the menacing block of tofu on the counter, and the herd of Japanese people moving past Susie Thomas, who still had her sky blue jelly shoes on. I fled. Susie followed fast behind me.

"Who were all those people?" Susie asked as we walked over to the old oak tree in my front yard.

"My mom's friends," I answered, dreading the next question.

"So, your mom speaks Chinese?"

"Japanese, actually," I said, correcting her.

"Do you speak Japanese?" She seemed interested to know.

"No, my brother and I never learned Japanese. Sometimes I feel like I understand what they're saying though," I explained, motioning toward my house.

"That's pretty cool. So you probably understand what they're saying in all those Bruce Lee movies?"

"Um, well, Bruce Lee is Chinese . . ."

Susie shrugged her shoulders. "Is your mom having a party or something?"

"She's having a meeting."

"Oh . . . for her work?" Susie's questions had a tendency to sound accusatory.

"Um, yeah." I decided to change the subject. "So, do you think Matt Brady will ask you to the dance?"

"Um, *yeah*," Susie said, mocking me, the inflection in her voice insinuating that everyone should know the answer to that question.

Remembering Susie's spiral notebook, which had "Susie Brady" scrawled all over its pages, I attempted to win her over and said, "If you guys got married, your name would be Susie Brady."

Susie beamed and said, "Susie Ann Brady."

"That's a pretty middle name."

"It was my grandmother's name. What's yours?"

"My middle name? Oh, it's Kim," I lied, without flinching. A middle name is such a small thing and yet, to me, it was paramount. It was something to keep hidden, something that, if revealed, would reveal something in me. "Kim," I repeated.

It began to grow dark. Suddenly a low, ominous hum, punctuated by a gong-like bell, swept through my quiet street. The hum got louder and louder, like something about to erupt. Words became audible. It was a chant, and it was coming from my house.

"What's that noise?" Susie asked, bewildered by this point and snacking on a premade package of cheese and crackers she found in her bag. She spread the malleable cheese onto each cracker with a plastic red stick. I decided to tell Susie the truth.

"Susie, I don't think we're going to be ordering a pizza tonight. They're praying. My mom's a Buddhist."

"Your mom's in a cult?" she asked incredulously.

Several days later, I awoke to the same chant, except this time it was only my mother's voice. I walked into her room, where she was kneeling before her *gohonzon*, a scroll of gold paper imprinted with Japanese characters that was housed very preciously in an upright black lacquer case. "The kids at school think you're in a cult," I said. She continued to pray, ignoring my interruption. "Why do you always have to pray?" She held her palms together, the jade beads laced between her fingers. "And why can't we have spaghetti more often? By the way, I don't like bringing leftovers for lunch, especially when they smell funny. Most people don't even bring containers to school. And I want to go to church like my friends. Why haven't you ever asked me what my religion is?" My mother tilted her head slightly to the left, but continued to pray. "You're always praying. If things are so hard, then why do we live here? Why don't we just move to Japan?" I waited for some kind of response, any response, really. "That stupid black box isn't going to bring him back!" My mother turned around and I felt a hand strike my cheek. Never in my life had I been struck. I felt my body quiver and a rush of blood run through every vein in my face. After a few moments, she looked at me and said, "Because this is your home."

I will never forget that day. That was when I began to realize that everything I had been so embarrassed about—my mother's religion, her language, her food, her culture—was a vital part of her, as important to the spirit as air is to the lungs, and as vital to her as she was to me. I looked again at my reflection. I was no longer thirteen. I had survived the embarrassment of tofu and dispelled the rumors that my mother was the leader of a cult. Yes, I was different. I didn't fit into a nice square box. I didn't even have a real box; I was "Other" with a line next to it.

Somewhere between thirteen and twenty-eight, it crept up on me . . . a sense of pride for who I was. The once-jumbled pieces of me had fallen into place. I looked closer. I had her eyes.

My thoughts were suddenly interrupted by a male voice. "Well, I think we got all of the confetti." I looked up and saw Dallas and my roommate holding two small trash bags. The flurry of color had disappeared from the floor. It was New Year's Day. Realizing that I had a very important engagement, I grabbed my coat and headed out the door.

The market was bustling that day. Pots of little yellow flowers and crates full of silvery red fish on ice were being brought in. The air was heavy with miso and pickles and the salty sea. The bakery had just opened and I saw my mother standing before the shining glass case, staring at the display of glistening pastries crowned with fresh cream. Without purchasing any, she made her way toward the candy aisle and picked up a package of Pocky, the cookies I used to love as a kid. They're long and dipped in chocolate and come in a colorful plastic cup. I walked up to the bakery counter. "Two, please," I said to the clerk.

Every year, my mother and I meet at the Japanese market in the city in celebration of *oshogatsu*, New Year's Day. Sometimes I pick her up, but she always complains that I drive too fast. I walked over to the candy aisle and approached my mother.

"Mom," I said. She turned around and smiled. I handed her the pink pastry box. Before opening it, her eyes grew wide and she asked in a half whisper, "Cream puff?"

We sat outside with our cream puffs and cups of green tea. I saw the joy in my mother's face and, somehow, I understood the joy that butter and sugar and cream could bring. It transported her back to a different time and place. I thought about the hours spent in prayer and the hope that it brought her. I thought about the way her voice changed when she spoke Japanese to those who understood her. I thought about what she had done for us, my brother and me, what she had given up for us, and everything she had given us.

"Mom?"

"Hmm?" my mother asked, watching a group of birds nearby. I noticed that one had strayed from the others.

"Thank you for giving me the middle name Kimiko."

She smiled and took my hand. "It means 'she who is without equal.'"

# THE HYPHENATED AMERICAN: ON CHECKING "OTHER"

Monica Villavicencio

> Too young am I and too outraged to be my freer self.
> —Kahlil Gibran, *The Forerunner*

I COMMITTED MY FIRST ACT of rebellion against "the system" when I was sixteen years old. It was too early on a springtime Saturday morning for the dreaded Scholastic Aptitude Test (SAT). I sat with sharpened No. 2 pencils, a ticking clock, clammy palms, and indelible etchings of fear and inadequacy.

The College Board acknowledges that there is more than one possible answer to any given SAT question, but that the trick of the test is to pick the "best" possible answer. Sitting the SAT is laden with weight and legitimacy, and every pencil mark on the Scantron page has an air of finality. And so it was with the race question.

*What is your ethnicity? Pick one from the categories below. White/ Caucasian. Asian/Pacific Islander. Native American. African-American. Hispanic/Latino. Other.*

I paused for much longer than I should have, thinking more than seemed necessary. Kaplan, the Princeton Review, and all the other standardized-testing sages urge us to eliminate the choices that we know are wrong and then pick the best possible choice out of what's left. And that's exactly what I did. I narrowed down, one by one:

> White/Caucasian—no
> Native American—no
> African-American—no
> Asian/Pacific Islander—yes
> Hispanic/Latino—yes
> Other—yes

At the end of the exercise, I had eliminated three and was left with three possible choices. And then I did what any well-trained eleventh grader would do: I blackened the bubble(s) for what I believed was/ were the best answer(s).

As a Nicaraguan-Filipina, I have my pick of answers, depending on the degree to which I'm feeling honest. Sometimes I'm "Hispanic." Sometimes I'm "Asian." There is no purpose or pattern to my answers; I don't alternate races/parents. In fact, it's all very arbitrary, and never fully accurate. If I wanted to be as precise as possible while adhering to the "check one" rule, I would have to check "other," but "other" is an ugly, meaningless word to me.

I was raised with my right hand over my heart, pledging allegiance to the flag of the United States of America. In elementary school each morning we sang: *My country 'tis of thee, sweet land of liberty, of thee I sing. Land where my fathers died, land of the pilgrims' pride, from every mountainside, let freedom ring!* My favorite holiday was Halloween, when I would dress up as a princess with a wand crafted of foil, or as a cat with a tail of stuffed black hosiery and a sack of candy. A number of my girlhood memories center around the handicrafts, nutrition education, and camping expeditions undertaken in the name of the almighty Girl Scout badge. I loved my chicken nuggets, and as far as I was concerned, I was American.

When I was nine, my family and I left our home in Los Angeles for greener pastures in London, England. It was the first time I'd stepped outside the familiar life of the American Catholic schoolgirl and entered an environment where I was identified by distinction. To my young mind, it felt strange that my use of strong and rounded *r's* and nasal *a's* was labeled an "accent." That my background, my identity, my way was not the standard or the norm was a notion wholly new and jarring. To be told that *I* was the one with the accent was strange. To me, water pronounced "woota" sounded foreign and accented. But I was the foreigner, defined by my otherness.

As children are wont to do, I quickly grew accustomed to the gray skies, damp air, and English accents. After all, for me it was all very exciting, being an American girl in England. The five years I spent overseas were punctuated with visits to family and friends in various parts of the States—Los Angeles, San Francisco, Miami, Washington, D.C.—and field trips to Greece and Spain and France and Italy. My family and I also journeyed to my father's region of Latin America to visit with family in Nicaragua and Honduras. Even with the special-guest treatment by my grandparents and aunts and uncles—complete with local delicacies like cow tongue and a well-orchestrated overnight trip to the beach—I found the streets of Managua, its dense heat and absence of high-rise buildings, unfamiliar and foreign. For my father, though, the trip was a homecoming; he even tossed around the idea of moving us back there, where we'd have a good, comfortable life—but my Filipina mother would hear none of that. Throughout my childhood, I saw home, family, and culture as distinct and separate phenomena that intersected only occasionally. By the time I was an early teen with a passport full of stamps, I was accustomed to the feeling of being foreign and didn't give a second thought to my otherness. In my mind, although I hadn't spent more than several weeks at a time in the States in five years, I knew that I had a permanent home across the Atlantic.

It wasn't until I returned home to the States at the age of fourteen that I realized that my identity, the nationality I had carved out in my mind, had been too simple. My Filipina mother and Nicaraguan father gave me dark hair, a petite frame, and almond eyes. Teachers and classmates took an interest in my "exotic" look and would often ask about my background, especially given my Spanish name and Asian features. It was always variations on the same theme: "Where are you from? What are you?" Selecting from my registry of answers, I'd oblige. "I moved from London." Or "I was born in San Francisco." Or "I'm American." Or, when I was feeling indulgent, "My mother is Filipina and my father is Nicaraguan." To which people would respond, "Where?"—meaning Nicaragua. And I'd explain that it was a very small, Spanish-speaking country in Central America. I became a very fascinating multicultural specimen indeed.

My first year in high school, I acquired a new vocabulary for identifying myself. I had left the States too young to understand the intricacies of race identification. I had left as an American. But as a teenager, I began to see myself through the prism of race. I was "mixed" and "biracial." I am smaller than most Americans; my eyes and nose are too Western to be Asian, my size and coloring too Asian to be Western. I am pale and thin, but my hips are curvy and my butt is round and full. My Spanish name doesn't fit with my face, which looks somewhat Asian with a dash of the West. I am not quite Asian, not Latina enough, and not as American as apple pie.

I am semiliterate in the language of Nicaraguan and Filipino transplants. I enjoy a good *carne asada*—a grilled, sliced steak popular in many Latin American countries—from time to time, washed down with a cold glass of *pinolio*, a Nicaraguan drink of milk or water mixed with baked ground corn kernels and unsweetened cocoa. And when my mother fries up some *lumpia*—Filipino spring rolls filled with vegetables and meat—and cooks *pancit palabok*, a Filipino noodle dish with seafood, onions, and pork rinds, I eat no fewer than three helpings. My travels have brought me to my parents' homelands, where I've taken in the sights and smells and met my family. And of course, I was raised Catholic—Latin American and Filipino style—which means many Sundays spent in church, saying grace before dinner, and a sprinkling of Bible readings in the evenings. Like the good Catholic Nicaraguan-Filipina that I am, I can recite the Lord's Prayer and Hail Mary, and I can tell you exactly what moments to stand, sit, and kneel during the weekly one-hour mass.

In this era of culture as fashion, I love how I am immediately exotic. I love how I can claim to have grown up in a tricultural environment. I love how people are always curious about my "ethnic" background and interested in how such a union came to be. I love it when people tell me that it's a good combination. My favorite thing, however, is when people lean in, as if admiring the work of a talented, innovative artist. I love to feel like a work of art. With the explosion of Latino culture into mainstream American media and the recent trend of Chinese characters tattooed on bodies and printed on t-shirts, my mix is in vogue. Who wouldn't want to be in vogue?

Although I can claim with pride that I am not just "American," a timid voice nags at my conscience when I take credit for being multicultural. This voice, soft but persistent, calls me a sham, a phony, a fraud. We speak English at home. My parents watch *Seinfeld*. But they think American culture is too individualistic, and couldn't understand why I wanted to live on my own before marriage. If I am really Latina, why is my Spanish grammar embarrassingly bad? Why is my accent halfway between Latina and American? If I am really Filipina, why did I have to learn about the Philippines from a chapter in *The Rough Guide to Southeast Asia?* Why don't I have any Filipino friends? Why does my family, on both sides, not really see me as one of them? Why am I American to my Nicaraguan and Filipino relatives and Nicaraguan-Filipina to my fellow Americans? How can I feel like all of the above and none of the above all at the same time?

These are the questions that eat at my pride, chomp away at my sense of culture until I am left with this half-eaten sandwich that doesn't really taste like much. Most fluent in American culture, I cannot forget that I am made up of other cultures, too. I look in the mirror, and the history of my features is an incessant reminder of this fact. Beyond that, I am faced with the expectation that I am not "just" American; inquiring minds hunger for an answer that will satisfy their appetite for exoticism. Worse still, I have the very same appetite, and I, too, long to be more than just American. Sometimes I feel proud to be interesting and diverse, but that pride is always shattered when I see "real" Filipinas and "real" Latinas—whose families embrace the language and culture of a foreign land. I suddenly feel less authentic.

I long to fit into one of the six racial categories the government has outlined because, even though they are just designations, somehow it matters to me. Perhaps I am searching for authenticity. I am proud to be "mixed," but I am afraid that my inability to fit into a category makes me culture-less.

And while I receive positive attention for what appear to be diverse roots, I have confided in a few friends that I envy their ties to a culture, whether it's Korean, Indonesian, or Mexican. Their response is understandable: *Why can't you just see it as having two cultures?* But I don't have a response. All I know is that I oscillate between feeling like a Renaissance woman and a Jill of multiple ethnicities but master of none. I swing and sway but have yet to make my peace with the cultural straddle and how to be all of the above and American, too.

Regardless of labels and categories and allegiances, culture is a feast of norms, values, and traditions that are shared. Culture is a structural framework; it is learned and passed down and its products are put behind glass cases in museums as works of profound beauty. Culture is community, and my inability to fully grasp and give shape to what culture is to me leaves me feeling lonely sometimes.

And although I often feel pale and watered-down, I rarely share that information with others. In fact, most of the time I talk about bits and pieces of my home life, snippets of my childhood that render me "colorful." My paternal grandfather refuses to speak English beyond his oft-repeated two words: "Spanish, please." We play salsa and merengue at family weddings. I have been to Asian supermarkets with my mother and watched her smile at the ingredients that flavored her childhood in Manila. She'll pick up some fish sauce and something with coconut in it, and sometimes when I'm perusing the refrigerator for a late-night snack, I'll find an unrecognizable dish tucked away at the back of a shelf, maybe something orange with an unmistakably strong smell of vinegar and fish sauce. My nose will crinkle up of its own accord. My mother has seen me and my brothers and father react this way, and that's why her special dishes are often savored in private. I wonder if culture is a lonely thing for her, too. We never talk about it in the family. It's as if culture is an irrelevant fact. I don't tell them how I feel, what growing up as a "mixed" girl in America is like, and it seems that it doesn't cross their minds to ask. My parents don't talk about their countries or cultures much these days.

Sometimes, though, I have moments of redemption. I used to work at Nordstrom with a short, prickly-haired thirtysomething Filipino named Ricardo. We bonded immediately over talk of *lumpia*, adobo, and my mother—Ricardo with his Tagalog-laced accent and me with my unabashed Americanisms. When another Filipino joined the Nordstrom staff, I was delighted. All three of us from that blessed Pacific archipelago bonded as we straightened racks of boys' clothing at a mall in suburban northern Virginia. To be taken into the fold of this Filipino "community" was a novel comfort. I was even told I had "good Filipino values." I never bothered to ask what that meant because it hardly mattered to me. Recognized and categorized, I happily obliged.

My better judgment moves me to stand up and defy categorization. I ask myself why it matters, why it should matter, why it doesn't not matter. The whole thing feels nonsensical, and yet, just because we all live together and work together and ride the bus together does not mean that race is not a strong identifying force in American culture. A lunch hour spent in many American high schools will reveal that voluntary social segregation along racial and/or cultural lines is commonplace. Applications for jobs, schools, and Social Security cards ask the race question. Affirmative action requires racial identification. The very structure of contemporary American society and the very definition of the American population invariably incorporate characteristics of race and culture. And so even if I tried to be just American, America doesn't work that way.

And so with sweaty palms and my fingers wrapped tightly around a perfectly sharpened No. 2 pencil, I attempted to grapple with that race question on the SAT. They say to pick one, but I elected to pick two. *Hispanic/Latino* and *Asian/Pacific Islander*. Perhaps it's the most honest answer I have ever given, but I had to break the rules to do it.

# BACK IN THE U.S.S.R.

### Victoria Gomelsky

THE LENGTHY QUEUE AT THE Aeroflot counter in New York's Kennedy Airport doesn't surprise me. Russians have a way of making even the most basic logistical procedures enormously complicated: forms filled out in triplicate, documents stamped *just so*. They can also be brusque, cold, and a little bit crazy. As I shuffle along, I wonder how many times I will see these sides of the Russian character in the month ahead.

Don't get me wrong. I'm proud of my Russian heritage. Unlike most tourists, who travel to experience the foreign, I am going half-way around the world to experience the familiar. My family lived in St.

Petersburg back when it was still called Leningrad; we emigrated as part of the Soviet Jewish exodus in 1978 when I was five years old. This trip marks my first return.

From the moment I join the queue, I suspect that I'm in for one long homecoming. I recognize my relatives in the faces of the passengers in line. The women have wide, round Slavic cheekbones; light, almost transparent eyes; and straggly eyebrows, which my grandmother, Tamara, and my mother, Natasha, have passed on to me. As they slink toward the Aeroflot desk, the men with their hairy chests and black mustaches remind me of all the dozens of Russians that have visited my parents' house over the years, downing vodka shots and dancing drunkenly to sentimental folk songs before leaving again, not to be seen for another decade. Do they look at me and think I am one of them? If they were to speak to me in Russian, they would be disappointed. Like a dog, I understand the language but don't speak it. At least not well enough to fool anyone.

It's clear that my seatmate, Victor, is Russian long before he opens his mouth. His pale, round face and nonexistent eyebrows are dead giveaways. When he learns that I was born in Leningrad, he strikes up a conversation with me in Russian. My garbled consonants and tortured sentences don't impress him. He says that language is only useful as a way to communicate. He says it kindly, but refuses to continue speaking with me in Russian, though I ask him to help me practice.

Instead, he offers to share his Ambien. Before the drug knocks me into a deep, dreamless slumber, I learn that he was born near Novosibirsk, in the middle of Siberia, but now lives in Detroit, where he works in the finance department at Ford. The work bores him to death, but he survives the grind by throwing himself out of an airplane every weekend. With 1,500 jumps to his credit, he is a professional skydiving cameraman. He's also a champion BASE jumper, meaning he gets his real thrills by regularly parachuting off towers and bridges. These feats allow him just eight seconds of freefall before impact.

"How do you know when to pull the chute?"

"I usually wait till I'm scared and then I give it another second," he says.

"That's crazy."

"No—what's really crazy is people who live their entire lives without ever testing their limits."

Ten hours later, I wake from the blackness of an Ambien sleep feeling giddy. It was an unexpectedly easy rest. I suggest that Victor and I exchange email addresses—he has invited me to watch him compete at the BASE jumping world championships at Moscow's Ostankino tower on the July 4th weekend—but he tells me we already did that. The drug worked a little too well.

My grossly overstuffed blue Samsonite has not exploded all over the conveyor belt when I go to pick it up at baggage claim. We are in Terminal 3 of Moscow's Sheremetyevo Airport and I must get to Terminal 1 to catch my domestic flight to St. Petersburg. The smells of cigarettes and of freshly baked piroshkis from the corner kiosk mingle in a way that reminds me of home.

But the aggressive taxi drivers in the central waiting area quickly dispel that soothing feeling. One offers me a ride, shoving a price list in my face despite my weak protests. We haggle briefly because I don't have the energy to argue, settling on fifty dollars (dollars are the currency of choice among members of Moscow's infamous "taxi mafia") for the journey to Terminal 1, which I give the man as he hustles me into a waiting car. It's an obscenely high price, all the more so when I discover that it takes less than ten minutes. Welcome to Russia.

I arrive in St. Petersburg in mid-June, just as the white nights are getting whiter. The city is located so far north that from mid-June to mid-July, the sun never falls deep enough below the horizon for the sky to get dark. Other places in the northern hemisphere experience the same phenomenon, but only in St. Petersburg have the white nights (*"Beliye Nochi"*) earned such acclaim.

I am here to attend a monthlong literary seminar. But in truth, the program is just an excuse. My real intention is to find my roots, although I can't help thinking this statement should have ironic quotation marks around it. How else to explain this vague quest to understand where I am from?

My spartan dorm room at the Herzen Inn, an aging hostelry located stumbling distance from Kazan Cathedral and the grand thoroughfare of Nevsky Prospekt, has seen better days, but it is safe and clean. I share it with a Kenyan writer named Andiah, who has a habit of sleeping late every morning and missing her fiction workshop. Of course, this first week we are all getting to bed rather late because it's impossible to drag ourselves away from the bars when the sky is bright and people are out enjoying themselves (and when jet lag has rendered us insomniacs). "Midnight in St. Petersburg is like lunchtime in L.A.," says Artyom, a banker whom my mother's best friend, Natalya, has put me in touch with. He is thirty-six years old, a lifelong resident of St. Petersburg, and the only real Russian with whom I have a connection.

Family members don't count. My parents read Russian newspapers, eat Russian food, speak the Russian language, but after twenty-six years in the United States, they are poster children for the American Dream, especially if you consider how they live, surrounded by all the trappings of an American existence: a house in the suburbs of Los Angeles, a Mercedes SUV in the driveway, Caribbean cruises over the holidays.

No doubt my fraternal twin sister, Julie, and I hastened their integration. As kids, we wanted nothing to do with Russia. My grandmother's thick accent embarrassed us. As did the smell of meat *kotleti* frying on the stove top, as did anything that betrayed our feelings of otherness. All we wanted was to be like our American classmates in Cherry Hill, the southern New Jersey suburb where we temporarily settled. When Jul and I entered kindergarten at the local elementary school in January 1979, we discovered the advantages of assimilation.

Having mastered English (by osmosis, it seems, because I don't recall a single lesson), we were soon playing tetherball matches during recess instead of loitering along the fence. We became friendly with Tara Elliot and Kim Edler, the popular girls in class. We earned shooting-star stickers on homework assignments. Above all, we blended in. This effort to maintain a seamless American lifestyle extended to our routines at home. Within a few weeks, we were answering our parents' questions in English and signing birthday cards as Vicky and Julie, not "Vika *ee* Yulia." We watched TV fiendishly, devouring episodes of *The Six Million Dollar Man* and *Welcome Back, Kotter* like we devoured the boiled potatoes our mom served us for breakfast. Soon, our Russianness, at least outwardly, was reflected solely in our last name.

It wasn't until college that my feelings about Russia began to change. When I was little, I would have done anything not to be different. As an adult, I began to realize that the differences are the only things that make me special.

My first week in Russia passes in a blur of jet lag and aimless wandering. The architecture of St. Petersburg makes my heart swell. It's a delirious mix of baroque, art nouveau, constructivism, Russian Orthodox, you name it. The enchanting onion-domed Church on the Spilled Blood, named after the spot where Czar Alexander II was assassinated, is located a few blocks from where I'm staying, so that I can hardly escape the sight of it. Every time I see those psychedelic spires in the distance, a smile springs to my lips.

One night, the program directors organize a midnight boat ride along the Neva River, where locals flock during the summer to see the nightly opening of the bridges, which are a ubiquitous presence in this city built on islands. Peter, as the Russians call it, was spruced up in 2003 for its 300th birthday celebration. When we glide through the maze of canals that have earned it comparisons to Venice, I notice the fresh paint. "A city of grand facades" is how Artyom described it. From the deck of the boat, where we drink cheap beer and wave hello to the raucous party cruisers that pass us, I see what he means. The gilded eighteenth-century edifices that stand along the canals conceal courtyards full of trash and the pervasive stench of urine.


All over the city, flyers announce what every local should know by now: Paul McCartney is going to play his first-ever concert in St. Petersburg in Palace Square on the evening of the summer solstice. This is a very big deal. Russians are huge Beatles fans, probably because during most of their lives, the music was forbidden.

On the day of the show, I stop at the central ticket office to inquire about prices and learn that tickets have ballooned from around 600 rubles, or about $20, to more than 3,000 rubles. That settles that. Instead, I decide to buy myself lunch at Quo Vadis, the Internet café that's been my home-away-from-home-away-from-home this week. Just as the waitress serves my steaming bowl of borscht, which I have loved since childhood, I overhear two young women greeting each other. One asks the other how she's doing, and the first woman replies, *"Ne ploho."* "Not bad"—as I have heard my parents say a million times. It's a classic, if banal, example of Russian pessimism. Things are never "great" like they are in America, because in Russia misfortune lurks around every corner. Think of it as self-deprecation without the irony. The only thing that alleviates the Russians' firm belief in inescapable hardship is their fatalism—the sense that whatever happens is supposed to happen. This reminds me of a joke my father once told me. At the height of the Cold War, when Americans were all busy building bomb shelters, Russians regarded their own mandated preparations with complete mockery. *What to do in case of a nuclear war: One, cover yourself with a white sheet and slowly crawl to the cemetery (so as not to create panic); or two, cover yourself with a white sheet and quickly crawl to the cemetery (to get a good spot).*

Eating borscht and listening to two pretty young women—each dressed in tight white pants and shockingly high heels—echo my parents underscores something I'm only now beginning to understand: All the traits, sayings, and customs I associate with my family—from the moments of superstitious silence we observe before leaving on a trip to the exclamation points that pepper our letters—belong to a larger cultural legacy I abandoned in childhood. Being here is my way of getting it back.

The borscht swishes around in my stomach as I make my way onto Nevsky, which has been closed to car traffic for the day. Something draws me to the barricades set up near the Moyka River crossing. Police are checking tickets before they allow people to enter the concert venue. The sky is filled with storm clouds that don't bode well for the open-air show. They contribute to a subdued, slightly uneasy vibe among the throngs of onlookers milling up and down the wide avenue. I snap a few surreptitious photos of the grim-looking officers who manage the barricades before I hear the voice of a scalper offering tickets for 300 rubles.

Without hesitation, I hand him my money. And then I am in, following a group of well-to-do Russians (even 300 rubles is pricey for a city where the average monthly salary doesn't exceed 3,000 rubles) into Palace Square, a stark expanse of pavement that fronts the Winter Palace, as beautiful as it is daunting.

A huge stage has been constructed behind the Alexander Column, the 155-foot monument built to celebrate Napoleon's retreat from Moscow in 1812. A group of people hug the stage, but the wide square feels conspicuously empty. Sir Paul is singing "Maybe I'm Amazed" to a lackluster audience. For a moment, I have to suppress my irritation at the Russian people. Can't they at least clap?

Not sure where to plant myself, I follow a blond wearing a powder blue tank top with a pale yellow raincoat tied around her hips. When she stops, I stop. She begins to sway to the music. Her movements are drunken: Her hips move from side to side with an aggressive shake, even when the sad songs come on. She and her friend, another blond with her hands in the air, are the only two people dancing, or even moving.

The sun emerges at around 9:00 PM and this stirs the crowd. Timidly at first, the concertgoers begin to loosen up and shed some of their earlier inhibitions. Thirteen years after the fall of the Soviet Union, an aura of authoritarianism still settles upon public gatherings here; it's as if people are waiting for permission to speak. By the time the band strikes up "Hey Jude," the mood has improved considerably. People are dancing, yelling, woo-wooing. The back of the square has filled with bodies, and the sun, bright and high in the sky despite the late hour, gives off a surreal lavender light.

To my left stand two middle-aged, mustached men. One of them has the classic Russian moon face, hidden behind a pair of sunglasses. It takes me a second to understand what's wrong with this picture. His frames are missing a lens, making him look slightly deranged.

His taller, red-headed companion approaches me and introduces himself as Volodya.

"Shall we dance?" he asks, the vodka on his breath thick and sour.

"Why not?"

We do a little jig. As we spin around in circles, he asks me where I am from. Slowly, I tell him that I am originally from St. Petersburg but now live in New York.

"Really? I can't believe it," he says, obviously delighted at the prospect of chatting up an American girl. "My cousin's friend lives in New York. What are you doing here?"

Conversation is difficult due to my poor Russian, but Volodya doesn't seem to notice. Every now and then, he turns to Vadim, his deranged-looking and equally drunken friend, and says something incomprehensible, inciting giggles from me. What a pair. Just when I think my smile can't get any bigger, Paul McCartney launches into "Back in the U.S.S.R." I feel as if he is singing it for me.

At the end of my first week in St. Petersburg, I go to dinner with some friends from the program, American writers trying to make sense of this country. On more than one occasion, I have heard them say the Russians make them feel "shut out" and "unwelcome."

How can I convince them that, in this city of grand facades, the scowls on the faces of the people they encounter on the street are only an exterior? It's true that the people of St. Petersburg don't go out of their way to make strangers feel welcome. Russians consistently rank low in studies on human happiness, and this is evident in their glum, even hostile expressions. But the moment they sense you understand something of their culture, they open themselves up to you. It happened to me after I thanked a clerk at the local convenience store using a few polite Russian phrases. Her expression softened and she quietly admonished me for not wearing a jacket, *didn't I know it was cold outside?* I tell my friends that if they get to know the Russians, they'll find they are among the warmest and most soulful people on earth.

To test this, I explain, they just need to sit down to a meal. The real essence of the Russian character emerges at the dining table, amid heaping plates of blinis, black bread, smoked sturgeon, cabbage piroshkis, meat cutlets, and *pelmeni* (boiled Siberian dumplings stuffed with ground beef and served with generous spoonfuls of *smetana*, or sour cream). This is when the public inhibitions are laid to rest. Fueled by the ever-present bottle of vodka, conversation continues well into the night. It is not unusual for a Russian dinner to begin at 8:00 PM, for the main course to be served past midnight, and for the last guests to depart by sunrise.

By the frustrated looks on my companions' faces, I know my words are falling on deaf ears. I can't convince them that just because Russians aren't as flamboyantly hospitable as, say, the Italians, they are anything but cold. And then it hits me: Russian culture isn't something tourists can easily embrace. But for insiders like myself, that's part of its charm. The Russians are not easy people to get to know, but once you get past the facade, they are delightful, crazy, delightfully crazy.

When it's time to go home, everyone else opts to walk the twenty minutes back to the Herzen Inn. But it's nearly 4:00 AM and I'm tired, so I hail a gypsy cab.

The driver is playing a dark, thumping techno-trance song that quickens my heartbeat. Instead of going around the block, he throws the car into reverse and zooms backward for about a hundred yards, giving me yet another glimpse of why people have described Russia as a wild place.

The Russians have a word for living on the edge—tempting fate and doing so with a secret, sly thrill. It is called *udal* and the fact that it is essentially untranslatable makes it all the more delicious. Here in this taxi, at this strange hour when the sky swirls with streaks of light and dark, I feel hungry for it.

"Are you Russian?" the driver asks, casting his eyes into the rear-view mirror.

"*Da . . . no toje Amerikanka,*" ("Yes, but also American.") I say.

His silence prompts me to say more.

"My family lived in St. Petersburg," I say, avoiding the more obvious phrase "I was born in St. Petersburg" because of the difficulty I have in pronouncing the word "born." *Radeelas.* "When I was five years old, we moved to America."

"You're ours then," he declares, reading my mind.

# ACKNOWLEDGMENTS

Thanks, first, to the women whose words grace these pages. Without you, this book wouldn't exist.

This book was buoyed by the guidance and encouragement of many. Thank you to Brooke Warner for insightful feedback and generous support from start to finish; Laura Didyk for coming in at the eleventh hour and helping me resee; Marisa Solís for her careful eye during the final stages; Leslie Miller for getting the project off the ground; Jenna Land Free for putting the bug in my ear; and Alle, Diane, Janis, Michelle, and Soula for all the rah-rahs over snacks and drinks (special thanks to A., D., and M.).

This project was inspired by my family on both sides of the Atlantic. I'm forever grateful to my mother and father and their siblings for the stories they've told throughout the years. Those stories are this writer's beginnings.

Lastly and always, thanks to Philipp, who feeds me and makes me laugh.

# ABOUT THE
# CONTRIBUTORS

**Amy André** is a graduate of San Francisco State University, where she received a master's degree in human sexuality studies in 2004. She is the vice president of, and sales-staff trainer at, Good Vibrations, the famous women-owned pleasure retailer based in San Francisco, where she has worked since 1998. In addition, she serves as a member of the board of directors at New Leaf: Services For Our Community, a nonprofit organization dedicated to the health needs of LGBT people in the Bay Area. Amy's interests include bisexual activism and fostering political development of the bisexual community. In her spare time, she does freelance writing and lecturing on women's sexuality, pleasure, and health, and on identity politics. For more information, please visit www.AmyAndre.com.

**Angela M. Balcita's** work has appeared in the *Florida Review, River Styx,* and in *The Fourth Genre: Contemporary Writers of/on Creative Nonfiction.* She is the recipient of the Eda Kriseova Fellowship in Nonfiction. She is currently completing her MFA in nonfiction writing at the University of Iowa.

**Marlene Barberousse-Nikolin** grew up in Chicago and south Florida. She currently lives in San Francisco and works in a sex-toy co-op. She enjoys reading, writing, Thai food, and photography, and she plays poker like a fiend. She wants to grow up and be a rock star.

**Jenesha de Rivera** is also known as Jinky by her friends and family. A native New Yorker and once a cosmetic chemist, she now spends her time helping nonprofits manage their finances. Primarily a fiction writer, Jenesha also enjoys writing personal essays and is currently dabbling in acting and writing for the stage. Her practice in the dharma and her long commitment to racial, gender, and economic justice inform her craft. She recently moved to Oakland, California, after thirty-three years of living in New York. Although she misses home and her family, the sight and smell of wildflowers blooming in March may keep her in the Bay Area. This is her first published piece.

**María Elena Fernández** was born and raised in Los Angeles, the daughter of Mexico City immigrants. She walked the straight and narrow academic path, attending Catholic schools, Yale University, and then UCLA for graduate school. Finally finding her way to writing, she became a poet, essayist, cultural critic, and performance artist. She has published extensively in the *LA Weekly*, has an essay in the anthology *Urban Latino Cultures*, and has performed her poetry and solo performance, *Confessions of a Cha Cha Feminist*, throughout the Southwest. She also teaches Chicano studies at California State University at Northridge.

**Laura Fokkena** grew up in Iowa and lived in Europe and the Middle East before moving to Boston, where she currently lives with her husband, Connor, and her daughter, Rakaya. Her writing has appeared in *Hip Mama*; *Egypt Today*; *YM*; *Home Education Magazine*; *Brain, Child*; AlterNet.org; PopPolitics.com; the anthologies *Expat: Women's True Tales of Life Abroad* and *Mamaphonic*; and other publications. She is also a member of the editorial collective at *Dollars & Sense*. She and her cousin, Heidi Sandler, recently completed *Wanderlust*, a family memoir exploring German American immigration.

**Margaret Gelbwasser** is a freelance writer based in New Jersey who focuses on writing about health and cultural issues. She is currently working on a novel, inspired by her own background, about three generations of one Russian Jewish family. The story begins in pre-Stalinist Russia and concludes in the present-day United States, and follows the evolution of the characters' relationships through the decades.

**Victoria Gomelsky** is an editor and freelance writer living in New York City. Her work has appeared in the *New York Times*, the *Philadelphia Inquirer, Escape, Hemispheres, The Sun*, and the *San Diego Union-Tribune*. She was born in St. Petersburg, Russia, in 1973 and emigrated to the United States in 1978. In 2002, she earned an MFA in nonfiction writing from Columbia University.

**Rasma Haidri** grew up in Tennessee and now lives on the Arctic coast of Norway. She has also made her home in Hawaii, Wisconsin, and France, and has spent time traveling on the Indian Subcontinent. She has completed a collection of meditative poems on the ocean and a chapbook of poetry covering the themes of her childhood. She has translated a book by the Norwegian poet Terje Johansen, and several works of prose by other Norwegian authors into English. Her writing has appeared in anthologies from the Chicago Review Press and Pudding House, among others, and journals such as *Nimrod, Prairie Schooner*, and *Kalliope*.

**Anne Liu Kellor** lives in Seattle, Washington. In 1996, she went to China for the first time, and since then has spent many years traveling back and forth between China and the United States. She is currently an MFA candidate at Antioch University in Los Angeles and is working on a collection of essays that explore cultural identity, spirituality, human relationships, and modern China.

**Tina Lee** is an angst-filled native San Franciscan who enjoys mild weather and her book club. She is a proud graduate of Mills College, where she obtained her BA in political, legal, and economic analysis with an emphasis in economics. She is also an inaugural-year graduate of the college's Lokey School of Business. Prior to becoming an account executive at a recruiting firm specializing in the IT industry, Tina had been a retail sales representative, a receptionist, a legal secretary, a director of business development for an Asian American–focused start-up magazine, and a management consultant, respectively. Tina has three younger siblings and resides in Oakland, California, with four plants. She'd eat the chip off her shoulder if only she weren't on a diet.

**Maliha Masood** is a writer, filmmaker, and activist. She is the author of *In the Middle of the East* to be published by Cune Press in 2005. She has also coproduced an award-winning documentary, *Nazrah*, featuring American Muslim women from the Northwest. Maliha earned her master's degree in international affairs from Tufts University. She is the founder of Dialogue on Islam, a nonprofit cultural institute based in Seattle, Washington.

**Rosie Molinary** earned her MFA from Goddard College. Her master's thesis, entitled "giving up beauty," focuses on exploring her coming-of-age through the lenses of ethnic identity, beauty perception, and body image. She lives in Davidson, North Carolina, where she writes and teaches creativity and writing courses through her business, Raise Your Voice. Her poetry and nonfiction have been published in *Jeopardy Magazine*, *Anthology*, *The Circle*, the *Rockford Review*, the *Her Mark Datebook*, the *Davidson Journal*, and *Yesterday's Laundry*, and in the anthologies *Coloring Book* and *Body Language*.

When **Sona Pai** and her husband, Mike Schurke, traveled to India for their monthlong honeymoon, Mike got sick after the one morning he chose scrambled eggs instead of *idlis* for breakfast, and Sona slipped and almost fell into the Ganges River. Sona received a master's degree in literary nonfiction writing from the University of Oregon and works as a freelance writer and editor.

**Jenny R. Sadre-Orafai** writes both poetry and prose. Her poetry has appeared in a number of publications, including *Wicked Alice, Poems Niederngasse, SubtleTea, Lily, Verse Libre Quarterly, can we have our ball back?, Red River Review, FRiGG,* and *Plainsongs.* Her prose has appeared in *Rock Salt Plum.* In spring 2005, Sadre-Orafai's chapbook manuscript, *Weed Over Flower,* was chosen for publication in Finishing Line Press's New Women's Voice Series; it will be available in fall 2005. Sadre-Orafai has hosted numerous open mics in addition to competing in slams. She has also recorded a spoken-word album. She currently lives in Atlanta, where she is at work on an MFA at Georgia State University. Ms. Sadre-Orafai is also an instructor of English at Kennesaw State University.

**Melissa Secola** earned her bachelor's degree in cinema at the University of Southern California's world-renowned School of Cinema-Television. She went on to study modernist fiction at University of Cambridge's International Summer School, English Literature Program. Her essay "The Opera Singer's House" appears in the anthology *Italy, A Love Story.* She lives in California.

**Lisa Swanstrom** earned a master's degree in creative writing from the Professional Writing Program at the University of Southern California, where she won an AWP Intro Journals Award for Creative Nonfiction. Her manuscript "The Leaping Bavarians and Other Stories" recently won first place in *Terminus Magazine's* annual chapbook competition. Other work has appeared in the *Mid-American Review, Nidus, Closer Magazine,* and *Moxie Magazine.* She also coedits the online literary journal *Sunspinner* (www.sunspinner.org) with Ellen Margaret Lewis. Lisa is currently a doctoral student in comparative literature at the University of California, Santa Barbara. You can find more of her work by visiting her personal web page: www.lisaswanstrom.net.

**Lan Tran** has more library cards than credit cards, loves traveling to places where you're not supposed to drink the water, and knows how to jimmy a parking meter. She has published fiction, creative nonfiction, and poetry in various literary journals. Her work has also been featured on NPR and produced at numerous off-Broadway theaters as well as at New York City Hall. "How to Unravel Your Family," her one-woman show, played to a sold-out audience at the American Living Room festival, sponsored by Lincoln Center Theater. Lan also likes food that no one else likes to eat.

Born and raised in California, Patricia Justine Tumang left the West Coast for New York City, where she received a BA in cultural studies with a path in race, ethnicity, and postcolonialism from Eugene Lang College in 2001. Her commitment to social justice and antiracist feminism from a queer Filipina American perspective permeates her life, writing, and activism. Her essay *"Nasaan ka anak ko?:* A Queer Filipina-American Feminist's Tale of Abortion and Self-Recovery" appears in the anthology *Colonize This! Young Women of Color on Today's Feminism* (Seal Press, 2002). She now resides with her partner in Oakland, California, where she is earning her MFA in creative writing from Mills College.

Monica Villavicencio currently lives in Washington, D.C. She has worked in media, education, and the nonprofit sector and will begin a graduate program in social anthropology this fall in the U.K. She enjoys reading, traveling, cooking, writing, and riding buses.

Emiene Shija Wright, twenty-seven, of Detroit, Michigan, is a writer/editor with seven years' experience in academic, magazine, and book publishing. Identity and its consequences are underlying themes in most of her writing. She was born in Jos, Nigeria, and grew up in the South and the Midwest, graduating from the University of Michigan with a bachelor's degree in English in 2000. She married in 2002. A passionate traveler, she counts Rome, Dakar, and Toronto among her favorite cities.

# About the Editor

Angela Jane Fountas is a writer, editor, and creative writing teacher. Her work has recently appeared in *Diagram, Pindeldyboz, Syntax,* and *The Writer,* and her story "Lydia" was nominated for a 2004 Pushcart Prize. She maintains WriteHabit.org, a website in support of emerging writers, and is working on a collection of short stories. Angela holds an MFA in creative writing from the University of Alabama. She lives with her husband in Seattle.

# Selected Titles
# from Seal Press

For more than twenty-five years, Seal Press has published groundbreaking books. By women. For women. Visit our website at www.sealpress.com.

*Under Her Skin: How Girls Experience Race in America* edited by Pooja Makhijani. $15.95, 1-58005-117-0. This diverse collection of personal narratives explores how race shapes, and sometimes shatters, lives—as seen through the fragile lens of childhood.

*Autobiography of a Blue-Eyed Devil: My Life and Times in a Racist, Imperialist Society* by Inga Muscio. $15.95, 1-58005-119-7. The newest manifesta from the bestselling author of *Cunt*, this time tackles race in America.

*Colonize This!: Young Women of Color on Today's Feminism* edited by Daisy Hernández and Bushra Rehman. $16.95, 1-58005-067-0. This diverse collection of some of today's brightest new voices takes on identity, family, class, and the notion that feminism is one cohesive movement.

*The F-Word: Feminism in Jeopardy* by Kristin Rowe-Finkbeiner. $14.95, 1-58005-114-6. An astonishing look at the tenuous state of women's rights and issues in America, this pivotal book also incites women with voting power to change their situations.

*Trace Elements of Random Tea Parties* by Felicia Luna Lemus. $13.95, 1-58005-126-X. Leticia navigates the streets of Los Angeles as well as the twisting roads of her own sexuality in this crazy-beautiful narrative of love and *familia*.

*Nervous Conditions* by Tsitsi Dangaremba. $14.95, 1-58005-134-0. With irony and skill, this novel explores the devastating human loss involved in the colonization of one culture by another.